Brandenburg, Beer & Brunch
Your Guide to a City Break in Berlin
By
Yvonne Salisbury

Copyright
Copyright © 2012/18 by Yvonne Salisbury.
All Photos © 2012/18 by Yvonne Salisbury.
First Published 2012
Last Updated October 2018
All rights reserved. No part of this publication may be reproduced in any form without the written consent of the copyright owner.
The author has done her best to ensure the accuracy and completeness of this guide, all prices and information correct at the time of publication, but things are always subject to alteration. Travel always comes with uncertainty and no travel guide can erase all of it, therefore she can accept no responsibility for any loss, injury, or inconvenience sustained because of information in this guide.

THIS PUBLICATION IS WIKI FREE

INSIDERS' GUIDES

"You're not here for a long time, just a good time"
Printed and distributed by **Insiders' Guides**
For all guides in the Insiders Guides Series see www.insidersguide-online.com

Thanks

I would like to thank my husband Stephen for taking me to Germany in the first place. Also, to family and friends who have supported me through this and my other works and, Nick and Jill, who have visited Germany with us and always joined in so enthusiastically with the research.

Preface

Say Berlin and most people think of the Wall, but there is much more to Berlin than just the Wall. It is a city with almost 800 years of history. Berlin is a vast, fascinating city and a monument of living history, where East meets West and old meets new. This is a city that staged a revolution, was headquartered by Nazis, destroyed, divided in two and finally reunited – and that was just in the 20th century! The Berlin Wall was dismantled in 1989, but the East and West districts still display signs, for now anyway, of the cultural divide that existed between them for almost 30 years. Berlin is not stifled by its past, it is pushing forward with shiny new developments and trendy bars to attract the young crowd. There is plenty to see; historians will enjoy the remnants of the wall, Hitler's Bunker and the new Jewish Synagogue Centre; culture lovers will enjoy the many of the 170 museums, galleries and theatres and if that is not for you then there is shopping, palaces, sports, festivals and great outdoor space. Berlin has something to offer everyone; here everyone can find their own Berlin.

Did you know that more than 15 of the German National Tourist Boards "Top 100 Sights in Germany" are here in Berlin? They are: the Brandenburg Gate, Potsdam and Sanssouci Palace, the Berlin Wall, The Fernsehturm and Alexanderplatz, Unter den Linden, the Berliner Dom, Museumsinsel, Reichstag, Gendarmenmarkt, The Ku'Damm, the Kaiser Wilhelm Church, KaDeWe, Berlin Zoo, Schloss Charlottenburg, Potsdamer Platz, Checkpoint Charlie, the Berlin Philharmonic Hall and the Jewish Museum.

As Berliners say "Komm'Se 'rin, komm'Se ran…" or "if you come, you will see…"

Contents

Berlin
Weather
History
Berlin and the Third Reich
The Berlin Wall
The City Today
What to See and Do
Festivals and Events
Shopping
Food and Drink
Planes, Trains and Automobiles
Useful Information
About the Author

Berlin

Berlin has been the German capital on several occasions throughout its history. Starting out as the capital of the electorate of Brandenburg, this city on the River Spree later became the capital of the kingdom of Prussia and then the German Empire. East Berlin was the capital of the German Democratic Republic. Since German reunification in 1990, Berlin has once more been the capital of Germany. It is a large city, by international comparison; the German capital is the second largest city in the European Union in terms of its population and the fifth largest in terms of its area.

Berlin is an evolving city, with new buildings joining the old across the skyline every day. With 175 museums, Berlin has museums to cover all interests from history to technology, from currywurst to spies; it also boasts over 50 theatres and approximately 300 cinemas as well as the numerous sights of historical interest. Berlin also has a relaxed vibe and lots of open spaces for a breath of fresh air. No city in Germany is greener than Berlin with its forests, lakes and sprawling parks. This laid-back way of life can be found throughout the city. When the weather gets warmer, life in Berlin moves outdoors to the beach bars, pavement cafés and open-air cinemas and theatres – perfect for enjoying the sunshine and the balmy summer nights. There are over 4000 bars, cafes and restaurants – so something to offer every palette and pocket. Festivals appear on the calendar throughout the year to entertain the locals and visitors alike.

Weather

Berlin has continental climate with mild spring and autumn, cold winters and warm summers. It is not unusual for sub-zero temperatures and long periods of frost during the winter months. From May to September the temperatures usually range between 15 and 25 degrees but on occasion can reach 30 degrees.

History

Berlin is a young city in historical terms, first being mentioned in a city document in 1237. At a natural ford in the River Spree, (the Mühlendammbrücke today), traders and merchants founded settlements on both sides of the river. These two merchant settlements, Berlin and Cölln, soon established themselves as the dominating trade and market place in the Brandenburg March, thanks to their outstanding strategic position on the river. They later merged and formed the city and the Nikolaiviertel is considered to be the birthplace of Berlin. In 1280 the city adopted the coat of arms it still has to this day, the Berliner Bear.

In 1415 Friedrich I began 500 years of Hohenzollern dynasty rule which continued until Wilhelm II in 1918, in the 18th century they also became Kings of Prussia and in 1871 the name Kaiser was added to their titles. Elector Frederick II laid the foundation stone for the Berlin Stadtschloss (City Palace) on the Cölln Spreeinsel (Island in the Spree), which later became the permanent residence of the Hohenzollern dynasty in Brandenburg.

In 1618 the 30 Years war had a devastating effect on the city with over half of the houses and buildings being destroyed. Frederick William offered asylum to the Huguenots in 1685, with over 6000 becoming residents of Berlin, and by the end of the century the city had a true multicultural feel with over a quarter of its citizens French, Poles and Czechs. The city became the capital of Prussia in 1701. In 1709, as "King in Prussia", Frederick I united the towns of Berlin, Cölln, Friedrichswerder, Dorotheenstadt and Friedrichstadt into the capital and royal city of Berlin.

At the beginning of the nineteenth century, in 1806, Napoleon conquered Berlin but allowed the city to self-govern until 1871, when it became the capital of the German Empire.

In the 1800's saw the start of the Industrial Revolution in Berlin. At this time Edison's Electric light bulb was introduced, the first independent locomotive was built and companies we know today such as AEG and Siemens began.

Because of the "Greater Berlin Law" of 1920, Berlin became the largest industrial city in Europe. The fundamental human rights anchored in the Weimar Constitution, combined with personal freedoms, enabled the city to flourish as the cultural metropolis of the 1920s.

Of course, no one can ignore the role the city has played in the twentieth century before, during and after the Second World War. In 1949, the Federal Republic of Germany (FDR) took control of West Berlin and the German Democratic Republic (GDR) the East. Free access between the two sides was permitted until the Wall, which was originally only barbed wire, was closed in 1961. It was not until 1971, under the Four Power Agreement that restricted access between the two sides was permitted. The Wall eventually came down in 1989. Today, almost 30 years on, Berlin is no longer a walled city, but a world city. Since those days, millions of visitors have come to Berlin, Germany's capital city, to see this change for themselves.

Berlin and the Third Reich

It is impossible to discuss Berlin's history and not mention the period under Nazi rule. The 30th January 1933, the "Day of the Takeover", was celebrated by the Nazis with torch processions through the Brandenburg Gate. It did not take long before they began to deal with their political opponents by incarcerating them in the first concentration camps to be set up. The emergency decree signed into law by Hindenburg following the Reichstag fire in February 1933 suspended the constitutional fundamental rights to personal freedom, as well as the freedom of opinion, association and assembly. The passing of the Enabling Act by the Reichstag on 23rd March 1933 finally opened the way for the Nazi dictatorship.

Most of the buildings and landmarks were destroyed in 1945 but there are a few that remain and a few locations that are now known to the public.

The former Air Force Headquarters at the corner of Wilhelmstrasse and Leipzigerstrasse stands today very much as it did then, however today it is home to the Finance Ministry.

The site of the Führerbunker (Hitler's Bunker) where he remained until his suicide, just before the end of the war, has now been officially marked. The bunker itself is in a car park, close to the Jewish Memorial on Cora-Berliner-Strasse and can be identified by the sign below.

In Treptower Park you will find the Soviet War Memorial, with over 5000 soldiers buried here, it is the largest war memorial in Germany.

As you walk around the city you may come across "Stolpersteine" or "Stumbling Blocks". These are a series of memorials began by Gunter Demnig to commemorate the victims of National Socialism and to keep alive the memory of all victims including Jews, gypsies, homosexuals and dissidents who were deported and exterminated. These brass stones will be found in the pavement outside the house where a victim lived and each one contains only one name. There are 3000 in Berlin and each district contains examples.

Topography of Terror
Niederkirchnerstrasse 8
www.topographie.de
10am to 8pm Daily

Since 1987 a permanent exhibition at the site has been providing information to the public about the most important institutions of National Socialist persecution and terror. The documentary exhibition conveys the European dimensions of the Nazi reign of terror.

A place where terror is real, a place of remembrance and a warning from history, the "Topography of Terror" exhibition is located on the site where between 1933 and 1945 the principal instruments of Nazi persecution and terror were located: the headquarters of the Gestapo, the high command and security service of the SS, and from 1939 the Reich Security Main Office. Gestapo, SS and Reich Security Main Office on Wilhelm- und Prinz-Albrecht-Strasse tells you about these institutions and the crimes that were organised there. At five locations, photographs and documents illustrate the history from the time the Nazis took power until the end of the war.

A second permanent exhibition in the trenches excavated along Niederkirchnerstrasse looks at Berlin's role as the capital of the" Third Reich" and is open from spring to autumn. Exhibition panels tell the story of Berlin in the Weimar republic, Berlin under the Nazis and during the war, and the consequences of Nazi rule. The glass panels let you look into the excavations on the site.

The last well-preserved former Nazi Forced Labour Camp and the Nazi Forced Labour Documentation Centre, a department of the Topography of Terror Foundation, can be found at Britzer Strasse, and is continually being developed as an educational site with an exhibition and archive. During the Second World War it served as one of the more than 3000 accommodations throughout the city for forced labourers. The Documentation Centre on Nazi Forced Labour opened in the summer of 2006 on part of the historical grounds that once belonged to the camp and which today are protected as a monument. Since August 2010 the well-preserved "Barrack 13" has been open to the public, it was one of the first buildings to be built in the camp and held mainly Italian military and civilians. In the cellar many names and inscriptions from the detainees can be found and this is the only evidence that they were held here.

Jewish Memorial
Cora-Berliner-Strasse
www.stiftung-denkmal.de
Ranked a German National Tourist Board "Top 100 Sights in Germany"

Near to the Brandenburg Gate is the Memorial to the Murdered Jews of Europe. It is a memorial that can be approached and walked through from all sides, serving as a central place for remembering and reminding people of the Holocaust.

On an area of about 19,000 square metres, the architect Peter Eisenmann erected 2,711 concrete pillars of varying heights to create a grid-like structure. The environment is smooth yet uneven. Visitors can enter the structure from all four sides and therefore the wave-like shape of each side is seen in a different aspect depending on where you are.

The extraordinary design, which was revised several times, represents a radical approach to creating a monument. An underground information centre also complements the memorial, where visitors can learn about the victims of the Holocaust and the various places of horror.

Jüdisches Museum

Lindenstrasse 9 – 14
www.juedisches-museum-berlin.de
Daily 10am to 8pm (Monday 10pm)
Ranked in the German Tourist Board "Top 100 Sights in Germany"

The museum is a timeless monument to Jewish life and history in Germany. With over four million visitors since its opening on September 9, 2001 the Jüdisches Museum is a stunning achievement in the architecture of cultural identity, a lasting expression of Jewish presence and dislocation and above all, an attempt at reconciling, physically and spiritually, the meaning of the Holocaust into the memory and consciousness of the city of Berlin.

The exhibition comprises over 2000 years of Jewish history, from Roman times to the present day, arranged in sections documenting the development of Jewish life in Germany. The Museum first opened to the public as an empty building; over 350,000 visitors and Berliners came attracted by the building's aesthetic symbolism.

The building is characterised by its shimmering zinc-clad walls, irregular lines and a star-shaped zigzag ground design with light coming through asymmetric slits, reminiscent of brutal stabs, on the otherwise smooth façade of the building. Seen from the air, the shape is that of a lightning-bolt.

The latest addition to the building is the spectacular Glass Courtyard completed in September 2007. Known as Sukkah, from the Hebrew meaning Tabernacle, the steel supports of the glass structure are arched branch-like formations, referring to a social gathering. The museum, an independent Foundation under Public Law since 1999, is a venue for an ongoing cultural programme, which includes exhibitions, symposiums, events and performances, as well as an educational programme.

The first Jewish Museum opened in Berlin in 1933 on Oranienburger Strasse but the Gestapo confiscated its collections in 1938.

The Berlin Wall

Ranked in the German Tourist Board "Top 100 Sights in Germany"

Berlin was a divided city for nearly thirty years, a city with a wall running through its very heart. From 13 August 1961 until 9 November 1989, the Berlin Wall divided the city into East and West Berlin.

Today, across the city you can find traces of the Wall, its remains and memorial sites – the East Side Gallery, the Berlin Wall Memorial in Bernauer Strasse, the Berlin-Hohenschönhausen Memorial, a former Stasi remand prison, and the green Mauerpark.

The route of the Berlin Wall is even marked along some of Berlin's streets by a double row of cobblestones

East German police, border guards, military and other State Security Officers, erected the Berlin Wall during the night of August 13, 1961. It was a weekend and most Berliners slept whilst the border was closed. By early Sunday morning most of the initial work was done and the border to West Berlin was closed, the wall stretched over 160 kilometres.

Initially, the East German troops began to tear up streets and to install barbed wire as a barrier; this was to be followed very soon by the concrete wall. The Berlin Wall was expanded in stages into militarily secured exclusion zones of many sections. It ultimately consisted of inner and outer walls, a service road, patrol areas, signal gates and watchtowers.

The purpose of the Wall was for the East German government to prevent further emigration to the West, more than 2.5 million had fled between 1949 and 1961, and the government needed to protect its regime and the economy.

Although many in the West had expected steps to be taken to halt this emigration, few had predicted the building of a barrier such as this. The Wall separated families and friends and thousands lost their jobs.

On the 750th anniversary of the founding of Berlin, separate celebrations were held in East and West Berlin. In his speech in front of the Brandenburg Gate on 12th June 1987, US President Ronald Reagan demanded: "Mr. Gorbachev, open this gate. Mr. Gorbachev tear down this wall!". It took another 2 years before his call was answered.

In all, 171 people were killed or injured trying to escape from the East to the West between 1961 and 1989.

The 25th Anniversary of the Fall of the Berlin Wall
The 25th anniversary of the fall of the Berlin Wall was celebrated on 9 November 2014. Many special events and exhibitions to commemorate the anniversary of this historic event occurred across the city. Themes included the division of the city, the Cold War and the events leading up to reunification in 1989.

The Berlin Wall Documentation Centre

Bernauer Strasse 11
www.berliner-mauer-dokumentationszentrum.de

Situated at the original location on the Bernauer Strasse is a section of the Berlin Wall with border strip and watchtower. The site shows how the border facilities were built and gives visitors a lasting impression of the construction, which once divided the entire country.

Documentation Centre
The Documentation Centre was set up by the Berlin wall Association and aims to provide information on the history of the Wall, its impact and consequences. The exhibits in the Documentation Centre show the history of the Wall's construction and the circumstances of the divided city. From the tower, visitors have an impressive view of the preserved parts of the former border and the memorial in memory of the division of the city and the victims of communist tyranny. There are listening stations with original reports, witness testimonies, photographs and changing exhibitions.
Displays are also in English.

Chapel of Reconciliation
The Reconciliation Church which was located at this site, was destroyed in 1985, as it stood right on the no man's land "death strip". After the fall of the Wall, the Chapel of Reconciliation was erected on the foundations and the victims of the Wall are regularly remembered during church services.

Further expansion
The Berlin Wall Memorial and Documentation Centre is presently being expanded and extended around an exterior exhibition on the former Berlin Wall strip at the south side of the Bernauer Strasse as part of the anniversary celebrations. In 2010, as an important element, the "window of commemoration" was completed on the former Sophien Cemetery.

A Journey along the Wall

The full length of this journey is around 12.5 kilometres, so you may just want to do part of it or spread it over a few days. In the city centre, a double row of cobblestones and bronze plaques inscribed "Berliner Mauer 1961–1989" marks the former course of the Berlin Wall. If you follow the markings, you can explore the remaining traces of the border

Bornholmer Strasse
Some sections of the Wall, some lamps and the lane markings of the former border crossing point can be found here close to the Bösebrücke. The most interesting fact is however, that during the last years, cars were sold on the area of the former border crossing point; East German citizens had to wait for over 10 years for a new car in former East Germany. It was a dream for many East Germans to drive or even to get a Western car.

Mauerpark
Mauerpark near Bernauer Strasse is a popular place for relaxation and recreation in the densely populated district Prenzlauer Berg. Many unknown graffiti artists have painted the former Eastern section of the Berlin Wall.

Bernauer Strasse
Sections of the Wall can still be seen here today, and the emptiness of some of the Eastern areas gives the area its character. Here you will find the Documentation Centre, the Berlin Wall Memorial and the Chapel of Reconciliation.

Garten Strasse
As you walk along Garten Strasse some sections of the wall are still visible and a row of cobblestones marks where the Wall crossed the street.

St Hedwig's Cemetery
This is the oldest Catholic cemetery in Berlin and a section of the original wall can be seen here.

Walk along Liesenstrasse and you will come across the border crossing point at Chausseestrasse. Continue along Boyenstrasse down Kieler Strasse alongside the canal and towards the Veterans Cemetery.

Kieler Strasse Watchtower
An original watchtower

War Veterans Cemetery (Invaliden Cemetery)
The War Veteran's Cemetery was closed to all foreigners during time of the Berlin Wall and citizens from the East needed a special pass to enter the cemetery. After the fall of the Wall the cemetery was opened again and its wonderful tombstones available to the public. Some original segments of the Wall and the patrol road still exist.

As you follow the canal banks towards Adenauer Strasse you pass the crossing point of Invalidenstrasse.

Parliament of Trees
The Parliament of Trees against War and Violence is a memorial for the people who died at the Berlin Wall started by the artist Ben Wargin in 1990 on the former border strip. The centrepiece is the Parliament of Trees, a square of sixteen trees planted in 1990 by the prime ministers of the sixteen states in the unified Germany. This installation of trees, memorial stones, and various artists created original parts of the border fortifications, pictures, and text. The names of the 258 victims of the Wall are inscribed on slabs of granite. The only original part of this installation is the patrol track, as the Wall segments come from other places in Berlin.

You then walk past the Reichstag to the Brandenburg Gate, the symbol of reunification when the wall came down, along Ebertstrasse to Potsdamer Platz.

Potsdamer Platz
Ranked a German National Tourist Board "Top 100 Sights in Germany"
Today, life is bustling at Potsdamer Platz, every day thousands of tourists and Berliners come to this area to visit the cinemas, shops, galleries and restaurants. However, for more than 28 years the place was dead land in the city's heart and at night the lamps of the Berlin Wall lit up the Potsdamer Platz area to prevent East German citizens from escaping to West Berlin. After opening the border in 1989 the Wall was very quickly demolished and only some segments survived. In 1999, ten years after the fall of the Berlin Wall, the Berlin government demolished the remaining Wall at Potsdamer Platz.
The East German watchtower on Potsdamer Platz is one of the last historical relics to open to the public. The observation tower originally stood between the Brandenburg Gate and Leipziger Platz and served as a base for border guards to monitor the chaotic terrain at the former House of Ministries.
Construction of the massive watchtower began in 1966 and by the end of the GDR era, there were more than 200 of these towers along the Berlin border. The tower was staffed around the clock by two border guards.
In 2001, it was moved to its present location near Stresemannstrasse on Potsdamer Platz. Today, it is the only surviving watchtower of its kind.

Niederkirchnerstrasse
The concrete blocks in Niederkirchnerstrasse are some of the few remaining first sections that are still in their original locations.

Checkpoint Charlie
Ranked in the German Tourist Board "Top 100 Sights in Germany"
A short wall of bricks is the last original witness of the times at this well-known border-crossing point in the heart of Berlin. A replica of the former Western Allied guardhouse was erected on the original site on August 13, 2000.
The Museum at Checkpoint Charlie, founded by Rainer Hildebrandt, offers an exhibition about the Berlin Wall in the style of the 70s and has become a museum in the museum.

The 200 square metres of the "Black Box" at Checkpoint Charlie informs the public on the history of this most famous border crossing point. With the use of large-format photographs and numerous media stations, it not only illustrates the impact of the Berlin Wall on the history of Germany, but also the full international implications of the division of both Germany and Europe are clearly demonstrated.

East Side Gallery
This is the final stop on the tour. Nearby the Oberbaumbrücke was a crossing point. The Wall here is just over half a mile long and the longest preserved section of the Wall.

Here is another shorter walk you can do which points out some sites of interest.

Berlin Wall History Mile

The Berlin Wall History Mile is a permanent exhibition in four languages. At 30 different stations along the Wall Trail inside the city, it tells the story of Berlin's division, the construction of the Wall, and how the Wall fell. The historical photos and texts describe events that took place at the location in question and highlight both the political situation and everyday life in the divided city.

Bornholmer Strasse
Describes how this area was a transport hub

Gleimstrasse / Schwedter Strasse
In Mauerpark this board describes life in the border zone

There are 4 in Bernauer Strasse each describing escape attempts:
Bernauer Strasse 48
Describes Ida Siekmanns failed attempt on 22 August 1961

Bernauer Strasse 78
Describes Tunnel 29

Bernauer Strasse / Ruppiner Strasse
The escape attempt of Conrad Schumann

Bernauer Strasse / Strelitzer Strasse
Tunnel 57 in which 57 people escaped but a border guard was killed

Gartenstrasse / Nordbahnhof
Describes Nordbahnhof as one of the "Ghost Stations"

Chausseestrasse / Liesenstrasse
This board shows the border opening in 1989

Sandkrugstrasse / Invalidenstrasse 1
Describes an escape attempt in 1963

Sandkrugstrasse / Invalidenstrasse 2
Here you will find details of Günter Litfin's escape attempt

Reichstagufer
Here you will see the White Cross Memorial

Ebertstrasse / Scheidemannstrasse
Here you find the Reichstag

Brandenburg Gate
A double row of cobblestones shows how the wall passed the Gate and it was also the location of President Reagan's speech of 1987

Ebertstrasse / Vossstrasse
Here you will find 3 boards describing life in a divided Berlin and Germany

Potsdamer Platz
Describes a city square on a border strip

Zimmerstrasse / Wilhelmstrasse
It was here that Ulbrichts speech in June 1961 declared, "no one has any intention of building a wall"

Zimmerstrasse / Friedrichstrasse
Here opposing tanks had a face off in 1961

Zimmerstrasse / Charlottenstrasse
This board describes Peter Fechter's failed escape attempt.

Zimmerstrasse / Jerusalemerstrasse
In the summer of 1962 a man successfully dug a tunnel to free his family from the East, a border guard died

Heinrich-Heine-Strasse
The locations of 2 escape attempts in 1962 and 1965

Waldemarstrasse / Leuschnerdamm
Here the board describes everyday life in West Berlin

Engeldamm / Melchiorstrasse
The canal to "no man's land"

Oberbaumbrücke
Here the 4 Permit Agreement was made to allow the West to visit the East for special occasions

May-Ayim-Ufer
Commemorates people who drowned or were shot trying to escape over the river

Pusckinallee
Here was a command post and the board describe the border fortifications

Harzerstrasse / Bouchestrasse
This board shows a map of the course of the wall and describes the impact the Wall had on the street

Sonnenallee Border Crossing
A row of cobblestones and photographs show crowds gathering at Easter 1972 before the 4 Permit Agreement was reached

Britzer Zweigkanal
Here you will find details of Chris Gueffroy's escape attempt in February 1989

The City Today

In 2001 the 23 boroughs of Berlin were regrouped into 12 districts, each with their own character and it is this character that gives Berlin it's beating heart. It is in these neighbourhoods that Berlin lives and breathes. Berlin's districts include old industrial areas that have become thriving cultural centres, as well as sleepy villages, busy markets and arcades, and endless green landscapes, rivers and bathing lakes. Above all it is the people who live there that make each neighbourhood unique. Just sit in the sun outside the cafés and restaurants and immerse yourself in the world of Berlins local neighbourhoods. Here is an overview of each district including some off the beaten track sights not always included in guidebooks. Full details of the main attractions are given in the next chapter on Things to See and Do.

Mitte

As the name suggests this is the centre or heart of the city, home not only to the Government but also many tourist attractions and landmarks all within walking distance of each other. The true vibe of the district can be felt around Hackescher Markt, an area totally renovated since 1990 and now buzzing with shops, bars and restaurants. The history of the city is represented in landmarks such as the Reichstag, the Siegessäule, the Philharmonic Hall, Bellevue Palace, the State Library and the Brandenburg Gate and today's modernism is reflected in the high tec of Potsdamer Platz. Other tourist attractions in Mitte are the numerous theatres, Museum Island and over 400 galleries. Alternatively, why not take a boat trip along the river here and see some of the sights from the water while relaxing with a drink in hand.

For shopping you have the grand tree lined boulevard of Unter den Linden, the arcades of Potsdamer Platz and the new shopping centres at Alexanderplatz.

Off the beaten track:

Gas Lantern Museum in Tiergarten Park
Tiergarten Park, located just behind Brandenburg Gate, is the green heart of the city. In winter, the historic gas lanterns along the paths in the park create a beautiful shimmering light and a magical atmosphere.
Carillon
The carillon in Tiergarten is well worth a visit. This unusual instrument comprising 68 bells is near the House of World Cultures in the north-eastern section of the park. The Berlin carillon is one of the largest in the world and played every Sunday from May to

September at 3pm and on some public holidays.
The Brown Bear Enclosure at Köllnischen Park
Since 1280, a bear symbol has decorated Berlin's official seal and coat of arms. However, Berlin's brown bear isn't just an emblem, the enclosure at Köllnischen Park, close to the Märkischen Museum, is home to three living examples of the city's mascot.
Meilenwerk
Wiebestrasse 36-37
Originally constructed in 1901 as Europe's largest tram depot, the Meilenwerk now hosts an exhibition of classic vehicles, from small cars to sport's cars.
Mon-Sat 8am– 8pm, Sun 10am –8pm
MountMitte
A high ropes course with many challenges located just behind Nordbahnhof station.

Charlottenburg- Wilmersdorf

The Kurfürstendamm (Ku'damm) is the centre of this district and an absolute must for any visitor to Berlin. From Breitscheidplatz, site of the Memorial Church, to Rathenauplatz with its concrete Cadillacs this district has a lot to offer; it is in its largest regeneration phase for decades with young and old fusing together in perfect harmony.

You can enjoy a wide range of sports in Charlottenburg-Wilmersdorf, you can go sailing on the River Havel, hang-gliding off Teufelsberg hill, rowing on the River Spree or swimming in the Hundekehlesee Lake. If you prefer walking, you can choose between the city, the many parks or experience nature at its best in Grunewald forest. Tourist attractions in this district include the Memorial Church, the Olympic Stadium, and Charlottenburg Palace. The Teufelsberg Hill was once a listening station during the Cold War and as well as tours of the station the hill offers fantastic views of the city.

For shoppers you have the 3.5 kilometres of the Kurfürstendamm or the world renowned KaDeWe. There is a great deal of nightlife in this area, the German Opera House, theatres, cabaret theatres, bars and restaurants and in the summer months many free concerts are organised by the Music Academy.

Rüdesheimer Strasse is one of the most beautiful streets in Europe, according to the New York Times. Rüdesheimer Platz is also without doubt one of the most charming sites in all of Berlin. In 1905, Georg Haberland designed the square, drawing inspiration from the English country house style. The houses are adorned with small front gardens, decorative façades and gables. Rüdesheimer Platz is the centre of the so-called Rheingauviertel. No wonder then that it is decorated with a large Siegfried fountain and wine queen

Off the beaten track:

Rüdesheimer Platz
In summer the wine fountain springs up on the square: Wine makers from the Rheingau serve wines in a small wooden hut. Residents and friends come with picnic baskets and savour the wine while sitting on the square, which transforms into a large open-air terrace.

Brixplatz
Just off Reichsstrasse in Westend, Brixplatz is one of Berlin's most attractive smaller parks and comes with a waterfall, little ravines, and a wild section of garden.

Amerika-Haus
The Amerika-Haus near the station Zoologischer Garten was built in 1957 as a culture- and information centre about the United States. Since 2010 the regional management of the City West moved into the monument and provides information about the economic and architectural development of the area around Kurfürstendamm.

Leonhardtstrasse
Located between the squares at Stuttgarter Platz and Amtsgerichtsplatz, this street has a great collection of independent shops and restaurants.

Das Verborgene Museum
Schlüterstrasse 70
The museum, founded in 1986, is dedicated to women artists who had already taken the first steps towards exhibiting their art to the public but were driven into exile or forced back into private life under the Nazi regime.

A-Trane
Bleibtreustrasse 1
Renowned among jazz fans as one of Berlin's top venues.

Friedrichshain-Kreuzberg

This fascinating district spans the River Spree and runs along the border of former East and West Berlin and these 2 former districts have merged together to give a lively and creative vibe to the area. The district's most well-known landmark is the listed Oberbaumbrücke Bridge with its striking towers and open-air gallery. A must for any visitor to Berlin is a stroll along the East Side Gallery, the longest remaining section of the Berlin Wall. Other attractions include the longest architectural monument in Europe, Karl-Marx-Allee and the Jewish Museum in Kreuzberg is one of the most frequently visited museums in Germany. Also, in this district are the state museum of modern art, photography and architecture and the German Museum of Technology with its large museum park, a natural oasis in the heart of the city.

Parks and riverbanks offer an attractive place for tourists and locals to spend some time. Visitors can enjoy fantastic panoramic views from Viktoriapark in Kreuzberg with its Schinkel monument. Friedrichshain's spacious public park with its fairytale fountain is popular among young families, athletes and tourists alike. Unforgettable views of Gründerzeit villas and ultra-modern buildings such as the Energie Forum can be enjoyed on a riverboat cruise on the River Spree and Landwehr Canal.

Shoppers can enjoy a stroll around the flea market of Boxhagener Platz in Friedrichshain or perhaps the quiet side street of Bergmannstrasse with its small stores and covered market.

Kreuzberg is renowned for its nightlife and street café culture, particularly around Oranienstrasse. On summer evenings there is a distinct relaxed Mediterranean feel with the smell of Italian and Turkish restaurants, bars and cafes late into the night.

Off the beaten track:

Kreuzberg's smallest house
Oranienstrasse 46
When in 1864 the Luisenstadt area was developed, a small terraced house was squeezed into the last plot of only 48 square metres (516 sq. ft), creating a unique building in Berlin. In 1991, this narrow house was largely restored to its original condition.

Lichtenberg

This is a district of contrasts, historical and modern, open spaces and culture, here you will find modern housing estates mixed with small villages, industrial areas and conservation areas. Young families and couples are being attracted to this area as new stores, cafes and galleries continue to open. There is plenty for visitors to see, Friedrichsfelde Palace is one of the most impressive baroque palaces in Berlin and the largest country park zoo in Europe, and Berlin zoo was founded here in 1955 in the landscaped Tierpark Friedrichsfelde. The Lichtenberg Museum can be found in Victoriastadt. The Taborkirche church dating from the 13th century is one of the oldest, smallest and most beautiful village churches in Berlin. History comes to life in

Lichtenberg: the German-Russian Museum in Karlshorst demonstrates the turbulent history between the two countries. The German Football Museum presents German football with all its international successes as part of a unique exhibition. While walking around the Kaskel area it is hard to miss the Schrotkugelturm (Lead Shot Tower), which reaches 40 metres in height and represents the lead shot that used to be cast there until the 1930's.

There is plenty of green space for you to enjoy and switch off from the noise of the big city: for example, at Barnimer Feldmark, Falkenberg Manor Park and the Dorfkate, as well as Malchow nature protection centre with its nesting storks. The areas around Obersee and Orankesee are popular for a gentle stroll.

Shoppers will find everything they could wish for at the Ring-Center on Frankfurter Allee or the Lindencenter on Prerower Platz. The Dong Xuan Center is Berlin's largest Asian market.

Off the beaten track:

Decorative support columns
In 2006, a residents' initiative in the Victoriastadt quarter created a remarkable memorial to 19th century rail engineering. The memorial colonnade comprises 12 decorative support columns rescued from the demolished rail bridge at Stadthausstrasse. The columns, designed by Hugo Hartung, were used on early rail bridges and overhead tracks in the city.

Herzberge Landscape Park
An area that was previously left to grow wild is now being transformed into a large central city park with trails for walkers, bikers and inline skaters. As it develops, this land will become organic fields and parkland where traditional Pommersche Landschafe sheep graze, and an ecosystem attracting rare birds and amphibians.

Pferdesportpark, Karlshorst
Here you can watch the trotting races, horse pulled two-wheeled carts. There are family days when you can have a ride in the cart and festival days that feature chariot races and camel racing.

Marzahn-Hellersdorf

This district is an area of contrasting architecture as well as green open space; here you will find the Wuhletal Valley, the longest corridor of green space in Berlin. The tourist attractions include The Gardens of the World in Marzahn, where you will find 100 hectares of beautiful landscaped gardens and the maze is popular with children. The Kiensberg Hill gives spectacular views of the city and a recent addition is the cable car that takes you from Kiensberg Hill to the Gardens of the World. The village of Alt Marzahn with its farmhouses stands unchanged for centuries and the best way to learn about the districts agricultural history is by visiting the Vom Korn zum Brot (from corn to bread) trail. This has an educational grain garden, an exhibition of farming machines, an animal farm, the district museum and cultural attractions. However, the highlight is without doubt the fully functional trestle windmill. The Gründerzeit Museum in Mahlsdorf manor house is furnished almost entirely in the neo-Renaissance style but if you prefer the outdoors then the Wuhletal Valley Trail is a well-signposted trail (16km) and a true paradise for keen walkers, cyclists and joggers. You can enjoy stunning views of Berlin's city centre and the surrounding region from the hills. The concerts in Biesdorf Park are a summer highlight.

For shoppers then the Eastgate Centre is a modern complex with over 150 stores and was voted Germany's best shopping centre in 2009.

Off the beaten Track:

Schloss Biesdorf
This late classical country house and tower date from 1868, and once belonged to the Siemens family. Recently refurbished it is now home to art exhibitions, the grounds with their attractive old trees, the park stage and the ice cellar are well worth a visit.

Neukölln

Rixdorf the historical area around which the district grew, with Richardplatz at the centre. Rixdorf was founded in the mid-18th century by protestant refugees from Bohemia. The historical buildings give you a good impression of what Berlin once looked like. The winding streets in old Rixdorf with their small shops and courtyards with vegetable and flower beds are more reminiscent of a village than a big city. Along Kirchgasse you can see the remnants of a Bohemian village from the mid-19th century. Amongst the tourist attractions are the Turkish Market at Maybachufer, Britz Castle and Gardens, the interesting streets of the Reuter and Rixdorf quarters, the Puppet Museum and the UNESCO World Heritage site of Hufeisensiedlung.

In the early 20th century the district had a less than favourable reputation and so firstly Kaiser Wilhelm II and then a local businessman, Frank Körner decided to revamp the area. In 1910, Körner gave to the district an area of gardens now known as Körner Park and today you can enjoy the gardens, fountains, and cafes and in the summer months concerts are held near to the orangery.

For shopping head to Gropius Passagen, Berlin's largest shopping centre, the Neukölln Arcades along the main shopping street or the Turkish Market at Maybachufer on Tuesday and Friday and the Neuköllner Stoff market with its designer goods on Saturday afternoons.

Off the beaten track:

Stadtbad Neukölln
Ganghoferstrasse 3
A visit to the Neukölln swimming pool combines relaxation with an architectural experience. The overall layout follows the design of Greek temples and basilicas, and the

two swimming pool halls, originally separated for men and women, are decorated with columned arcades and mosaics in a classical style. The Neukölln swimming pool is also a social meeting point for locals where after swimming they chat and relax on the gallery or at the marble basin under the columned walk near the pool.

Fraulein Frost
Ice cream parlour with traditional and more unusual flavours on offer.

Pankow

This trendy district is to the north east of Berlin and offers a mix of culture, nightlife and recreation. In the centre of Pankow is Schönhausen Palace, Berlin's newest museum detailing German history over 350 years, the Prenzlauer Berg area is particularly charming and has a renowned nightlife. KulturBrauerei is the place to be for art, culture and nightlife, covering an area of 25,000 square metres in an architectural monument. You can learn about German reunification with a guided tour around Gethsemane Church, Kollwitzplatz and the Mauerpark whilst Jewish life, past and present is represented by a visit to the synagogue on Rykestrasse and the Jewish cemeteries in Weissensee and on Schönhauser Allee.

For shoppers around the Schönhauser Allee arcades and Rathauscenter Pankow shopping mall, there are a wide variety of retail outlets for you to browse. You can also enjoy strolling along Kastanienallee and the streets around Kollwitzplatz and Helmholtzplatz are considered by many to be the best place to soak up the atmosphere of this district. The quirky shops in Prenzlauer Berg, with plenty of fashion, design and arts and crafts, ensure you will find the perfect memento of your visit.

Off the beaten track:

Prenzlauer Berg Museum
The local Prenzlauer Berg museum presents changing exhibitions on regional subjects. The museum apartment exhibits a typical 19th-century worker's flat, while Heynstrasse 8 shows how the middle-class lived at the same time.
Sundays in Mauerpark

The Mauerpark (Wall Park) has a large Sunday flea market with small stalls ideal for a browse. In the nearby open-air Amphitheatre, there is a free afternoon karaoke session, attracting hundreds of people to listen, join in or just chill out in good weather.
Botanical Gardens Pankow (Botanischer Volkspark Pankow)
From a teaching garden established in 1909, Pankow's botanical gardens now occupy 30 hectares with 6000 plants species, exhibition greenhouses, water and stone gardens and woodlands. One main attraction is a festival to celebrate the blossoming of the Queen of the Night at the end of June or in early July.
The Weisser See
In the heart of Berlin, there is a lake beach with clear water, palm trees, barbecue and bar plus fantastic sunsets against the shimmering light of the lake's fountain, and anyone who visits in winter can go ice-skating!

Reinickendorf

Just minutes from the city, this could be described as Berlin's green and blue district; green as in Tegel Forest and the countryside along the river and the blue of the Tegeler See and the River Havel. In Alt Tegel are Sechserbrücke Harbour Bridge and the Greenwich Promenade have landing stages for boats and cruise ships, from where you can tour Berlin by boat. The Tegeler See is a good place to hire a rowing boat, canoe or pedal boat in the summer and mess about on the lake for a few hours.

Lübars family farm is a great day out for the whole family. At the traditional Brandenburg farmhouse, you can learn all about the animals living here, as well as how to bake bread, make butter, process wool and lots more. In bad weather or during the winter months, there is endless fun and games for young and old alike at "Jacks Fun World", Berlin's largest indoor leisure park. Those with an interest in history and architecture are not forgotten in Reinickendorf, highlights include the former Borsig site with the listed Borsig tower and gate, where the "Hallen am Borsigturm" centre offers a combination of historical buildings and modern architecture.

For shoppers Reinickendorf offers a great range of shopping facilities such as Tegel-Center with its adjoining pedestrian precinct, the Hallen am Borsigturm and the Märkische Zentrum, each with around 120 shops. In Frohnau, Ludolfingerplatz has several traditional established specialist stores and various exclusive boutiques can also be found on Hermsdorf's Heinsestrasse and at Zeltingerplatz.

Off the beaten track:

Tegeler Fliess
The Tegeler Fliess stream runs through one of Berlin's most charming green areas, from Lübars to the Tegeler See Lake. The stream and banks offer a habitat for plants and animals in an urban environment. Hiking trails and a nature trail pass by nesting places for birds, rare flowers, thickets and trees.
The "Dicke Marie" Oak Tree
This oak tree, in section Jagen 74 of Tegel Forest, dates from 1192, making it not only

the oldest tree in Berlin but older than the city itself. Alexander and Wilhelm von Humboldt named the tree after their cook.

Chapel of Basil the Blessed

With its blue onion-domed towers, the Chapel of Basil the Blessed, a copy of the famous Moscow cathedral, stands at the centre of the Russian-Orthodox community's cemetery on Wittestrasse.

Teichstrasse Operating Theatre Bunker

In December 1941, the Nazis ordered a bunker with an operating theatre to be built. Today, the restored bunker can be toured and gives a vivid impression of wartime civil air defence and the bombing raids.

Spandau

The district of Spandau can trace its history back to the 7th century and is surrounded by countryside, forest and marinas and offers the visitor golf courses, walking trails and water sports. Spandau is probably most famous for its citadel and the Julius Tower, one of Berlin's oldest surviving buildings. The Gothic House and Museum offer an insight into the city's history.

For relaxation you can enjoy the parklands of Gut Neukladow with the old manor house, Villa Luise. The grounds are filled with trees and look down towards the River Havel. The Tiefwerder is known locally as "Little Venice", and you can explore the narrow waterways by rowing boat or canoe and look at the waterside gardens as you float gently by.

Spandau has the largest pedestrianised shopping area in Berlin with 3 department stores and more than 160 smaller stores. The old quarter offers traditional shops and from March to November there is a farmer's market four times a week.

Off the beaten track:

The Gothic House

The Gothic House was built in the late 15th Century as a residence and is the oldest secular building in Berlin. Today, many exhibitions and the Tourist Information occupy the building. The Spandau City Museum is situated on the upper floor.

Fort Hahneberg

It was built from 1882 till 1888 as the last artillery fort in Germany, yet due to the rapid development of technology it became obsolete before it was even completed. From 1952 the fort was situated on the borders to the East and was not accessible, this led to the whole ground lying waste. Today the fort represents itself as an architectural, military and nature monument.

Air Force Museum of the German Military, Gatow Airport

This could possibly be the biggest (in surface area) secret of the capital. The museum is an insider tip for two reasons: firstly, it is situated on the periphery of the city and secondly it has free entry. Hangars, the tower and former runways are the main components of the air force museum. There are over 100 planes and helicopters located in the open-air area.

Steglitz-Zehlendorf

The district of Steglitz-Zehlendorf, south west of Berlin, consists of seven suburbs: Wannsee, Nikolassee, Zehlendorf, Dahlem, Lichterfelde, Steglitz and Lankwitz. The good transport links connect the city to this leafy district that is full of recreation areas with forests and lakes, cultural highlights and remarkable attractions. Transport has always played an important role in this district as it was here in 1792 that the first paved road in Prussia was constructed and almost a century later the first electric tram came into operation.

The famous Glienicke Bridge where spies were once exchanged connects Steglitz-Zehlendorf to Potsdam on the other side of the River Havel. In nearby Glienicke Palace Park and on Peacock Island, which can only be reached by ferry, you can follow in the footsteps of the Kings of Prussia. The villa of the famous Berlin painter, Max Liebermann, is situated on the shores of Lake Wannsee and the nearby "House of the Wannsee Conference" memorial centre looks at the holocaust.

There is an impressive array of leisure facilities in the area with around 190 sports clubs, countless children's play areas, and both indoors and outdoor pools. The Grunewald Forest offers visitors the opportunity for quiet walks. The largest summer pool is at Wannsee as well as Berlin's oldest lakeside beach and the Wasserski Club offers lots for water sports enthusiasts.

Museum enthusiasts are well catered for here too; visitors can immerse themselves in foreign worlds and cultures at the Dahlem museum complex, which includes the Ethnological Museum, the Museum of Asian Art and the Museum of European Cultures. The world's largest collection of Expressionist works can be found in the Brücke Museum. Dedicated to the role of the western forces in post-war Germany, the Allied Museum is not only popular with American tourists. The museum village of Düppel contains an incredible reconstruction of an excavated medieval village. Demonstrations of traditional crafts are held here in the summer. You can witness farming life at its best at the Domäne Dahlem open-air museum, with traditional market events such as harvest festival and Advent markets.

Schlosstrasse is a boulevard with lots of shops, department stores and shopping malls, surrounded by pleasant cafés and bars and a very popular shopping area. Zehlendorf-Mitte has several smaller, individual shops for you to wander around. Flea markets are held on Sundays at Steglitz town hall.

Off the beaten track:

Die Königliche Gartenakademie – Horticultural Centre
In 1823, Peter Joseph Lenné, Berlin's most renowned landscape architect, founded the Royal Gardening School next to the Botanical Gardens; today it is a horticultural centre. The centre not only showcases the latest horticultural trends but also sells shrubs, accessories, pots, tools and garden furniture. Café Lenné, with its delicious food and snacks, is ideally situated in this green oasis for a well-deserved break during your visit here. The botanical garden itself is one of the most bio-diverse in the world. In addition to the Botanical Museum, it has more than 22,000 plants and a tropical house, which reopened in 2009 after refurbishment. A series of summer concerts are held in the gardens from May to September.

Tempelhof-Schöneberg

Tempelhof is a modern residential and industrial district whilst Schöneberg is a centre for the services industry with a colourful and diverse range of institutions. John F. Kennedy famously said the words "Ich bin ein Berliner" at Schöneberg town hall. Altogether, this is a lively district offering a combination of urban life and idyllic surroundings with many seemingly contrasting facets. For visitors to Tempelhof-Schöneberg, the journey into Germany's past begins here, taking you right through the district and various eras, from the airlift at Tempelhof airport to the site of the former Sportpalast. Famous residents include Marlene Dietrich, David Bowie and Billy Wilder; it is colourful and multicultural, combining a gay/lesbian scene with traditional life, greenery and history.

You can enjoy the entertainment on offer at the UFA-Fabrik, look through a telescope at the Sternwarte am Insulaner observatory, or see the places of remembrance in the former Jewish district around Bayerischer Platz. The energetic can enjoy roller blading along the 1.2 km stretch of historical railway line at the Hans-Balluschek-Park in Schöneberg's Südgelände nature reserve or climbing up Insulaner hill or simply taking a stroll in one of the many parks and green spaces. The district is home to one of the city's more unusual parks, located on the former Tempelhof airfield, at weekends you will find roller bladers using the runways, kite surfers on the taxi ways and families riding bikes and flying kites on the surrounding meadows. The Sultan Hamam is the largest Turkish bath in Germany offering relaxation for body and soul in the style of the Arabian Nights.

The largest department store on mainland Europe, the KaDeWe, can be found on Tauentzienstrasse. There are also plenty of shops to look around at Akazienstrasse and Winterfeldtplatz, where Berlin's oldest weekly market has over 250 stalls offers shoppers the chance to browse at cheeses, meats, fruit, vegetables and household goods. The district's latest addition is the 'Tempelhofer Hafen': the only shopping centre in Berlin with direct access to the water.

Off the beaten track:

Rathaus Schöneberg
The town hall dates from 1914 and between 1949 and 1991 it was the office of Berlin's Governing Mayor. During the years of Berlin's division, it witnessed some key events in the city's history. This was where the USA presented a Liberty Bell to Berlin in 1950 and John F. Kennedy gave his famous "Ich bin ein Berliner" speech in 1963.

Naturpark Schöneberger Südgelände
The Nature Park Schöneberger Südgelände has a mix of modern art and old railway installations where nature has been left to run wild. The former shunting yard in Berlin-Tempelhof has been transformed into a unique green landscape with relics from the steam age. After the shunting yard was closed, an area of 18 hectares was slowly left to return to nature.

Alter St.-Matthäus-Kirchhof
The Alte St.-Matthäus-Kirchhof cemetery was established in 1856 and is located between Grossgörschenstrasse and Monumentenstrasse in Schöneberg. The prominent figures buried here include the Brothers Grimm.

Hans Wurst Nachfahren
Founded in 1981, this professional puppet theatre is one of the most popular in Berlin. The puppet theatre is open all year and has a varied programme including fairy stories, own plays on current topics, literary adaptations, and evening shows for adults. The theatre works with a variety of puppet techniques.

Treptow-Köpenick

This district south east of Berlin stretches from the city centre to the surrounding countryside and is the ideal spot for a city break in Berlin or a fascinating excursion and just a few minutes from the city centre. 800 years of city history, important industrial monuments, a vibrant social life with shops, restaurants, culture and entertainment blend with ice-age hills, forests and parks. Rivers, lakes and canals turn the district into a dream destination for all types of water sports. The "Captain of Köpenick" is renowned for its special Prussian ambience.

Set on an island at the point where the Dahme and Spree rivers converge is the historic old quarter of Köpenick. The baroque Hohenzollern Palace houses the Arts and Crafts Museum. The Gothic town hall was where the mayor was once arrested and in 1906 the city's treasury stolen by the "Captain of Köpenick", known as the "coup of Köpenick", this event is documented in a small museum. The old quarter has numerous restaurants and cafés where you can pause for refreshments and many of them are on the water's edge.

Berlin's largest lake, the Müggelsee, is just a few minutes from the old quarter and is a delight for bathers and sailors. The beach bar adjacent to the boat jetty is popular all year round, in winter you can enjoy a warm drink around the campfire while in summer relax in a lounger under the sunshades sipping cocktails. Friedrichshagen, with its variety of restaurants, is located on the northern shores of the lake. Cruise boats operate services from the city centre to the Lakeland area. The Müggelberg hills are home to Berlin's highest natural elevation (115m) and are a popular destination for walkers, cyclists and bladers. There are several outdoor pools where you can cool off in the summer or go ice-skating in the winter.

Treptow Park offers several tourist attractions along the banks of the River Spree. It is home to the largest Soviet memorial in Western Europe, Treptow harbour with its passenger boats, the Archenhold observatory that has the world's largest refracting telescope, and the Zenner Inn with its riverside beer garden.

The "Forum am S-Bahnhof Köpenick "is the largest shopping centre in the south east of Berlin. There are smaller malls in Schöneweide and Treptow and the shopping streets such as Bölschestrasse in Friedrichshagen and the lanes of Köpenick's old quarter have retained a special atmosphere.

Off the beaten track:

Schesischer Busch Watchtower Headquarters
The tower is one of the two last preserved and accessible watchtowers of the GDR border troops. It was built in 1963. Since 1992 the building stands under monument conservation. Today the renovated tower reminds visitors of Berlin's separation and occasionally houses exhibitions.
Neu Venedig (New Venice)
In the 1920s and 1930s, canals drained the meadows around the River Spree; gradually a residential area with water sports facilities and gardens was created with almost as many harbours as permanent homes. Bridges connect the islands, but the best way to reach them and to discover this idyllic landscape is a boat tour.

What to See and Do

There is so much to see and do in Berlin; in fact, it is impossible to pick out a "Top 10". There are hundreds of museums and galleries, sights both new and historical, parks and gardens, the zoo and Sealife Centre, palaces and churches and numerous points of interest regarding the Third Reich and its effect on the city. Whatever you are interested in and however long you are here it is almost impossible to see it all.

Sightseeing Tours

These are always a good way to get your bearings in a city.

Bus 100 / 200
www.bvg.de

This is a public bus service that runs from Alexanderplatz to the Zoo and takes in many sights along the way including the Dom, The TV Tower, Siegessäule, the Reichstag and along Unter den Linden all at the low-cost price of a regular bus ticket. The website gives you details of the routes and departure times. The bus 200 runs a slightly more southerly route past the embassy area and Potsdamer Platz, both buses meeting on Unter den Linden. These bus routes are considered a good value option for seeing the city.

Hop on Hop off Bus
www.berolina-berlin.com

This is a tour I have used many times and I always take these tours whichever city I am in as I find them very useful for visitors to locate where the sights are and then you can come back and visit the ones of most interest in greater detail.

The tour of Berlin is available in 13 languages, has 20 stops around the city including all major attractions and lasts 2 hours. The buses run at 15-minute intervals starting at 10am and the last complete tour is at 3pm.

Boat Trips
www.reedereiwinkler.de

A boat trip is another way to see the city. There are 2 different daytime tours each lasting around 3 hours, a 1-hour tour and an evening tour, which includes dinner. You will pass many sights including the Dom, the Reichstag, the Zoo, Potsdamer Platz to name just a few. All tours provide a detailed description in English.

Berlin on a Bike (www.berlinonbike.de) offers cycling tours of the city and the price includes hire of the bicycle, or if walking tours are more your thing then try Berlin Walks (www.berlinwalks.com) who operate a number of different tours throughout the city.

Attractions

Top Tip:
The **Berlin Welcome Card** offers unlimited travel within the public transport network for 48 hours, 72 hours or 5 days. Tickets for the public transport network (S-Bahn/City Railway, U-Bahn/underground, tram and bus services) in fare zones AB (Berlin) or ABC (Berlin and Potsdam). You also receive a map and a guide with great savings of up to 50% on more than 200 top sights and cultural highlights:

36 top sightseeing highlights
27 museums & exhibitions
26 top attractions
40 theatres and shows
50 clubs and restaurants including some hotel restaurants
25 Potsdam highlights

Berlin Welcome Card including Museumsinsel (Museum Island)
Includes free admission to the Museums of the Museum Island on three consecutive days (excl. special exhibitions)
The card can be purchased at Tourist Information Offices, the main Central Station and

other transport hubs and over 200 hotels throughout the city. For more information see www.berlin-welcomecard.de

Brandenburg Gate
Ranked in the German Tourist Board "Top 100 Sights in Germany"

The Brandenburg Gate is probably one of the best-known landmarks of the city. It was one of 14 original city gates completed in 1792 by Carl Langhans and its design is based on the Propylaeum of Athens' Acropolis. The goddess of victory, Nike, drives the chariot on top of the gate, and it is from here that German armies have begun many a procession through the city over the centuries.

The gate was part of the Soviet sector in 1946 and in 1961 when the Wall was built, the gate was inaccessible to citizens as it stood in no-mans land. When the wall fell in 1989, 100,000 people gathered here for the reopening of the gate and since then it has become a focus for celebrations such as New Year, World Cup and football events when the street becomes pedestrianised and hundreds of thousands of people gather to celebrate.

The gate links the Strasse der 17 Juni with Unter der Linden and opens on to Pariser Platz, which today is an open square surrounded by elegant buildings and a must have photo opportunity. Since the Wall came down in 1989 the Brandenburg Gate has come to symbolise the unity of the city and country.

Reichstag
Ranked a German National Tourist Board "Top 100 Sights in Germany"

In 1894, after ten years of construction, the Reichstag was completed, and its dome towered above the city. Kaiser Wilhelm II, who was Kaiser Wilhelm's grandson and now in power, raged against this "pinnacle of bad taste." He discredited the architect, referring to the Reichstag as the "Reich's monkey house" and prevented the inscription "To the German People" ("Dem Deutschen Volke") from being inscribed on the façade, this was later added in 1916.

The Parliament building remained and, from that point onwards, it has reflected the turbulence of German history. On 9 November 1918, Deputy Philipp Scheidemann proclaimed from the window the creation of a republic. On 27 February 1933 under mysterious circumstances that still have no proper explanation, the Reichstag caught on fire, destroying the chamber and the dome. The fire served as a ploy for the Nazi regime to persecute their political opponents. In subsequent years the building falls into a state of disrepair.

The building was destroyed during the war and rebuilding began in 1961, in a simplified form without the dome. It has little ceremonial use during the next 3 decades other than for occasional art collections and an exhibition "The Questions About German History". After German reunification, the German Bundestag decided to once more use the building as the Seat of Parliament and continue to do so. Between 1994 and 1999, Sir Norman Foster redesigned the Reichstag as a modern Parliament building while retaining its extensive, historical dimensions. The glass dome, initially a controversial addition, has since become one of the landmarks of Berlin, entry is free, and you get the most fantastic views of the city.

Top Tip:
It is only possible to visit the dome by prior registration www.bundestag.de

Berliner Dom
www.berlinerdom.de
Ranked in the German Tourist Board "Top 100 Sights in Germany"

With its magnificent dome, the Berlin Cathedral is one of the capital's main attractions. With its elaborate decorative and ornamental designs, the church interior is especially worth seeing. However, although the church is known as a cathedral, it has the status of a parish church. This was the court church to the Hohenzollern dynasty, the rulers of Prussia and later the German Emperors. Although a church had stood here since the 15th century, in 1888 when Friedrich Wilhelm II became Emperor of Germany he decided a much greater building was needed, he wanted Berlins answer to St Paul's in London or St Peters in Rome. Several plans were submitted and in 1894 the foundation stone was laid, and in 1905 the building was consecrated.

During World War II, the cathedral suffered heavy damage and restoration began in 1951. During the division of the city, the Dom was situated in the East and restoration was stopped. The restoration was finally completed four years after the fall of the Berlin Wall in 1993. The golden cross on top of the dome was added in 2008.

Today you can see the church and its impressive cupola along with the baptismal and matrimonial chapels, the imperial staircase, and the Hohenzollern crypt with nearly 100 coffins dating back four centuries and the Cathedral museum. The Dom's organ with over 7000 pipes is a masterpiece and one of the largest in Germany. The museum displays drawings, designs and models illustrating the history of the Cathedral. You can climb 270 steps to the dome's outer walkway and be rewarded by some stunning panoramic views. The richly decorated Imperial Staircase was intended for the use of the German Emperor. The stairwell comes with an American-made lift included at the request of Kaiser Wilhelm II, an enthusiastic follower of new technology.

Rotes Rathaus
Rathausstrasse 15

The Rotes Rathaus is the town hall of Berlin and is the home to the governing mayor. The construction of the town hall began in 1861 and it replaced several smaller buildings dating from the Middle Ages and now occupies an entire city block. The name of the building comes from the facade design with red clinker bricks.
The building was heavily damaged during the war and rebuilt to the original plans between 1951 and 1956. The reconstructed Rotes Rathaus, then located in the Soviet sector, served as the town hall of East Berlin, while the Rathaus Schöneberg was seat of the West Berlin Senate. After German reunification, the administration of reunified Berlin officially moved into the Rotes Rathaus on 1 October 1991.

Fernsehturm
Panoramastrasse 1
www.berlinerfernsehturm.de
Ranked in the German Tourist Board "Top 100 Sights in Germany"

Everyone who has been to Berlin has seen it and it is no wonder - the Berlin Television Tower, which is 368 metres tall, is the tallest publicly accessible building in Europe. This is where an urban myth was created regarding the tower, all school children at that time were taught that the tower was 365 metres high (same as number of days in a year) so that it would be memorable for all, but it was later revealed to be another 3 metres higher.

The Berlin Television Tower, or the Berliner Fernsehturm, was opened on 3 October 1969 just before the 20th anniversary of the GDR and at the time it was one of the most important symbols demonstrating the superiority of socialist societies. The construction of the Berlin Television Tower showed that a better future was being built in the East.

While the GDR has long since gone, the Berlin Television Tower still stands, and it is now accepted as a landmark for all of Germany. Every year more than a million visitors from 86 countries go up 200 metres to the observation level and take in a breathtaking view of the ever-changing city.

The giant sphere's greatest moment of glory was during the World Cup Football Championships in June 2006 when it was transformed into a giant silver and magenta coloured football. It became the perfect symbol of the world football event.

Around the base of the tower are an exhibition centre and a restaurant building in a collection that includes the Neptune fountain, once situated on the palace square. The cascades are representations of four German rivers: The Rhine, Elbe, Oder and Weichsel.

Berlin Zoo
Hardenbergplatz 8
www.zoo-berlin.de
Ranked a German National Tourist Board "Top 100 Sights in Germany"

The zoo was given to the city in 1844 by King Friedrich Wilhelm IV of Prussia and is the oldest zoo in Germany. Perhaps the most famous image of the zoo is the magnificent Elephant Gate and its most famous recent resident was Knut the polar bear born in the zoo. Today it houses over 25,000 animals from over 2000 species in enclosures set in beautiful parkland and you wind your way through them along pathways and alleyways. The aviary is the largest in Europe. There are cafes, restaurants and shops for refreshments and souvenirs. The zoo is open every day.

Adjacent the Elephant gate is the zoo aquarium and tickets can be purchased separately for this.

Charlottenburg Palace
Spandauer Damm 10 -22
www.spsg.de
November – March, Tuesday to Sunday 10am to 5pm
April - October, Tuesday to Sunday 10am to 6pm
Ranked in the German Tourist Board "Top 100 Sights in Germany"

Originally it was built as a small garden castle for Sophie Charlotte, the wife of Elector Friedrich III and the main core of the structure, which was begun in 1699 and had the name of Lietzenburg Palace, was not particularly large. However, when Friedrich was crowned King of Prussia and Sophie Charlotte became his queen, it was then that the ever-increasing expansion of the palace began. After her death, aged 36, the palace was renamed after her and became Charlottenburg. Sophie was not the only Queen to love the palace, Queen Louise did also and is buried here with her husband. During the 18th century the palace was used less and less by the Royal family and in 1880 was no longer classified as a Royal residence.

During World War II, the palace was severely damaged, and the reconstruction work lasted two decades. Today it is an impressive ensemble of rooms and halls and is home to world-class art collections, including the largest collection of 18th century French paintings outside France.

The Silver Vault includes stunning tableware of gold, silver, glass and porcelain displayed on laid tables. Around 100 table services have survived intact, a vivid reminder of the magnificence of dining at court. The impressive display of the remaining pieces of the Prussian crown jewels, complete with the imperial insignias, as well as personal treasures, such as the elaborated designed, exquisite snuffboxes collected by Friedrich the Great, are also well worth seeing.

The palace gardens were originally created in the French baroque style but were later redesigned by the gardener Johann August Eyserbeck into an English style garden. Queen Sophie Charlotte loved strolling round the gardens and hosting parties here. In addition to other buildings, can be found the former Belvedere teahouse built by Langhans and the mausoleum containing the tombs of Queen Louise and Friedrich Wilhelm III.

Bellevue Palace
Spreeweg 1, Tiergarten
www.bundespraesident.de

Located in the Tiergarten, right on the banks of the Spree and close to the Victory Column, the Bundestag and the Brandenburg Gate, Bellevue palace is situated in the centre of Berlin.

The palace was commissioned by the younger brother of Friedrich II, Ferdinand of Prussia, and was completed in 1786. The building is simple in style but was surrounded by a large park which was one of the most beautiful Prussian landscape gardens. It was the fantastic view over the surrounding park that gave the palace the name "Bellevue". Several famous people stayed here during this time including Napoleon.

Several decades later, in the mid-19th century, the palace became an art museum and at this time the gardens were opened to the public. After a couple of decades, the artwork was moved out and employees of the Prussian Court such as cooks, gardeners and gamekeepers moved in.

After the first world war the palace was used to house state visitors. The building was destroyed during the second world war and rebuilt in the late 1950's at which point it became the second home of the President. Since the beginning of 1994, the Bellevue Palace has been the official residence of the Federal President and if the Federal President happens to be staying in Berlin, the standard of the Federal President is raised on the roof of the palace.

Siegessäule
Tiergarten
April – October, 9.30 m – 6.30pm
November – March, 10am to 5pm

"Golden Else," as the monument is known in Berlin, was built between and 1864 and 1873 and is now under a preservation order.

The 8.3-metre-high bronze sculpture, which was created by Friedrich Drake, represents Victoria wearing a helmet and holding a laurel wreath in one hand and in the other a staff bearing an iron cross. The victory goddess Victoria from Roman mythology is equivalent to the Greek goddess of Nike. The construction was to celebrate Prussia's victory in the German-Danish war in 1864, however during the years of construction two additional victorious wars were added: the German war of 1866 against Austria and the Franco-Prussian War of 1870. The founding of the German Empire is described in the bronze relief and mosaics around the plinth of the column.

During the era of National Socialism, the Victory Column increased in size to a total height of 67 metres. Between 1938 and 1939, in preparation for the future capital of the Reich, the Victory Column was moved to the middle of Tiergarten from its original location just in front of the Reichstag.

The viewing platform offers a wonderful panoramic view of Berlin. This is a favourite sightseeing trip with children who appreciate the view from the observation deck after climbing the 300 steps up the spiral staircase to reach the top. The Café Victoria and Biergarten, just next to the monument are ideal for refreshments and a break.

Kaiser Wilhelm Memorial Church
Breitscheidplatz
www.gedaechtniskirche-berlin.de
Everyday 9am to 7pm
Ranked in the German Tourist Board "Top 100 Sights in Germany"

The Gedächtniskirche or Kaiser Wilhelm Memorial Church is the symbolic centre of West Berlin. It was built between 1891 and 1895 in memory of Kaiser Wilhelm I, the first German Emperor. With 5 spires and the second largest bells in Germany, the church reflected the tastes and trends of that time and of the Kaiser himself.

Following allied bombing during WWII, the original west Tower has remained standing as a ruin and is hauntingly known as the "hollow tooth" as it is literally an empty shell. Immediately recognizable and located on the Breitscheidplatz at the start of the Ku'damm, this is the only building on the square that was spared by the rebuilding and has been deliberately preserved as a part ruin.

The Gedenkhalle (Memorial Hall) contains photographic exhibits of the Church and the surrounding area before and after the War. Other exhibits of interest are liturgical objects from bygone days and mosaics.

The Church remained heavily damaged until 1956 when the new building was built including an adjacent modern church, an octagonal hall and a bell tower. The controversial modern tower consists of an octagonal structure and a six-sided bell tower. Over 20,000 pieces of stained glass make up the walls of the modern Church.

The gift shop sells postcards, guides and souvenirs. The surrounding Breitscheidplatz area is a good place to sit in the open-air.

Olympic Stadium
Olympische Allee
www.olympiastadion-berlin.de
November – March, 9am to 4pm

March – May & September – October, 9am to 7pm
June – September, 9am to 8pm

The Olympic Stadium and Bell Tower (Glockenturm) was built for the 1936 Olympic Games. The original horseracing track built by Otto March was demolished in 1934 to make room for the new National Stadium designed by March's sons Werner and Walter March and supervised by Hitler's Imperial Interior Ministry.

Werner March's project for the 1936 Olympic Games, designed in typical Fascist monumental grandeur, was intended as a full-scale sports complex; an Olympic Square, an Olympic Stadium seating 110,000 spectators and a track field known as Maifeld which could also be used as a marching ground for mass rallies of up to 500,000 people and an Olympic swimming pool. The Waldbühne, one of Berlin's most popular open-air venues today, seating 25,000 was built for gymnastics competitions.

The Bell Tower is an iconic image that is renowned for its amazing views. The lift whisks you to the top of the tower for a panoramic view out across the nearby Maifeld and stadium to the city or over the Waldbühne to the woodlands beyond.

After the war, the site was reopened in 1946 when the British troops stationed in Berlin hosted an 8-nation track-and-field competition for Allied Forces soldiers. After the fall of the Wall in 1989, Berlin's bid for the 2004 Olympics failed and in 1998 the Berlin Senate took the decision for the full transformation of the former complex into a modern multifunctional sports venue.

A comprehensive renovation and modernization of the Stadium began at the turn of the millennium and was completed in 2004, as a multi-functional sports and events arena which can seat up to 76,000 spectators. On July 9, 2006 Berlin's Olympic Stadium hosted the FIFA Soccer World Cup final between France and Italy, the world's most widely broadcast event to date.

The Stadium and the exhibition in the Bell Tower carry vivid memories of the iconic images of American sprinter Jesse Owens whose historic four-medal Olympic victory shook Hitler's theory of the superiority of the Aryan race. The Bell Tower and Visitor's Centre with the German Historical Museum Exhibition on the ground floor, "Historic Site: The Olympic Grounds 1909 – 1936 – 2006", is open from April 1 to November 2 daily from 9 am to 6 pm.

A history trail on the Olympic site has 45 panels in English and German offering a fascinating insight into the complex's origins and development down the years, as well as information on the historical art works from the early years of the Nazi regime.

On event free days you can explore the stadium yourself or guided tours of the Olympic Stadium grounds are available daily and include the usually off-limits areas such as the VIP lounges, information points documenting the history of the complex and the locker and changing room areas of Berlin's Bundesliga Football Club, Hertha BSC. The stadium is easily reached on the U2 line.

The Story of Berlin
Kurfürstendamm 207
www.story-of-berlin.de

The Story of Berlin is the chance for you to experience the life of the capital over 800 years. Hear, see and smell history. The interactive exhibition allows you to cross from spectator to living participant with the aid of special lighting, slideshows, interactive touch screens and recordings. Each section has plenty to keep children busy and the younger ones will enjoy searching for the Berlin bears hidden in each theme room.

The exhibition begins in the 13th century, when the city was a trading centre and ends in the present day. The darkest period of Germany's history is not ignored; a special series of rooms show the grim nature of the Third Reich in a thought -provoking manner.

Highlights of the museum include the divided living rooms that give a glimpse into life on each side of the Berlin Wall, and the still functioning underground nuclear bomb shelter built by the city in the 1970's. Exhibition texts and the guided bomb shelter tour (every hour on the hour) are in English and German.

Museums and Galleries

Berlin has over 170 museums that welcome millions of visitors each year to their vast collections. On offer are unmissable artefacts such as the Pergamon's treasures of antiquity, the Jewish Museum. From Nefertiti's bust to a speck of the Wall at Checkpoint Charlie, Berlin's museums bring its unique character and history to life.

Top Tip:

You can buy a Museum Pass which entitles you to free entry for 3 consecutive days to over 30 museums including Museum Island, Jewish Museum, MachMit and the Labyrinth Kinder Museum.

Museum Island
Museum Island is a collection of 5 museums that has been declared a UNESCO World Heritage site. For opening times see www.smb.museum
Ranked in the German Tourist Board "Top 100 Sights in Germany"

The **Altes Museum** (Old Museum) is Berlin's oldest museum, originally opened in 1830, opposite the Lustgarten. It was built by Karl Friedrich Schinkel, Prussia's most influential architect to allow the public access to items of historical and cultural interest. Today it houses the Classical Antiquities collection, displaying a selection of it's with a selection of its Greek and Roman holdings.

The **Alte National Galerie** (Old National Gallery) was built between 1866 and 1876 and restored in neoclassical style by Friedrich August Stüler in the style of a Greek temple. The Museum reopened to the public after a thorough restoration in 2001. It houses one of the most important collections of 19th century painting in Germany and includes masterpieces by Claude Monet, Auguste Renoir and Auguste Rodin. Amongst the most important highlights are K D Friedrichs "Der Mönch am Meer", Arnold Bröcklin's "Die Toteninsel, Adolph Menzel's "Flotenkonzert Friedrich des Grossen in Sanssouci" and Edouard Manet's "Im Wintergarten".

The **Neues Museum** opened in 1859 to ease overcrowding in the popular Altes Museum. It was one of the most ambitious building projects of its time due to the use of new industrial construction technologies such as the steam engine. Built in the neo-Classical style, important Classical painters decorated the three exhibition floors, and the grand staircase winding through all three stories is a stunning focal point. Near the end of

World War II, the museum was severely damaged by bombing, and partially destroyed.

The building was left abandoned for decades, and restoration was only decided upon in 1985. Since 1997, British architect David Chipperfield has been charged with overseeing the renovation of the building as part of a general restoration of the entire Museum Island, which runs until 2015.

The Neues Museum will once again house the archaeological collections of the Egyptian Museum and Papyrus Collection, the Museum of Pre- and Early History, as well as works from the Collection of Classical Antiquities. The most prominent feature of the exhibit, the bust of Egyptian Queen Nefertiti, described as "the world's most beautiful woman," will be centrally and prominently displayed in the north cupola of the building.

The Pergamon Museum is one of the most popular attractions in Berlin and is world famous for its archaeological holdings. The Pergamon, is really three museums in one; the Collection of Classical Antiquities (also on display in the Old Museum), the Museum of the Ancient Near East, and the Museum of Islamic Art.

In the Collection of Classical Antiquities, the 2nd century BC Pergamon Altar, considered a Hellenistic masterpiece, has a frieze depicting a battle between the Gods and the Giants; the Market Gate of Miletus shows an important example of Roman architecture. The Museum of the Ancient Near East, which ranks among the world's best collections of treasures from this region, is dominated by the imposing bright blue glazed-brick Ishtar Gate of Babylon from 6th century BC. The gate is decorated with dragons, lions and bulls, symbolizing the major gods of Babylon; a transparent back wall lets visitors see how the massive gate was reconstructed from fragments. The Museum of Islamic Art began in 1904 with a donation of precious carpets by Wilhelm von Bode. Such textiles still make up a major part of the exhibition, with colourful examples from Iran, Asia Minor, Egypt and the Caucuses on view. Major restoration of the Pergamon is underway, but the museum will stay open throughout the process.

The Baroque **Bode Museum**, the fourth museum to be built as part of Berlin's Museum Island was completed in 1904. Intended as a museum for European Renaissance art, it was named after its first director Wilhelm von Bode (1845-1929) in 1956. Reopening to the public in October 2006, the museum brought together the sculpture and Byzantine art collection.

The museum's treasures include the sculpture collection with works of art from the Middle Ages to the 18th century. Of interest are the halls devoted to the Italian Renaissance with glazed terracotta's and other masterworks from Donatello, Desiderio da Settignano and works from the German late Gothic school. The Bode museum is best known for its Byzantine art collection and the coin cabinet.

Mauer Museum
Bernauer Strasse 111
www.berliner-mauer-dokumentationszentrum.de

April – October, Tuesday to Sunday 9.30am to 7pm
November – March, Tuesday to Sunday 9.30am to 6pm

The Dokumentationzentrum Berliner Mauer is a documentation centre dedicated to the Berlin Wall. It includes three elements: an authentic remaining stretch of the Berlin Wall, the Kapelle der Versöhnung (Reconciliation Chapel) and a Documentation Centre. For those interested in the Berlin Wall here is a vast amount of information and special documentation relating specifically to its historical and political background.

Admission is free, and this is an excellent opportunity for a great "Wall package" with the stretch of Wall accessible through a small park just opposite. The exhibition includes the chronological presentation of the events leading up to August 1961, when the Wall was erected, as well as a re-creation of the "death strip" between East and West Berlin where nearly 200 citizens lost their lives attempting to flee to the West. The re-creation includes the whole scenario of watchtowers, guards and guard dogs, barbed wire and mines required by what was known in East Germany as the "Anti-Fascist Protection Barrier".

German Spy Museum
Leipziger Platz 9
www.deutsches-spionagemuseum.de
Daily 10am to 8pm

The only museum of its kind in Germany here you enter the world of espionage and secret service. Learn about spy techniques, secret missions and hear former secret agents talk about their past lives. Among the objects on display are umbrellas with integrated poison arrows, gloves hiding a pistol and shoes with bugging devices in the heel. Touch screens allow you to view these bizarre objects from different angles. Have you got what it takes to be a spy? Test yourself on a laser course or at cracking a secret code.

Directly behind the German Spy Museum Berlin, you will see the last GDR "BT 6" watchtower from 1966. You can enter the tower itself and enjoy panoramic views of the former border area

German Historical Museum
Unter den Linden 2
www.dhm.de
Daily 10am to 6pm

The museum takes you through 2000 years of German history, from the Middle ages to the present day. Presented in chronological order you walk through the exhibits which can switch between art or objects such as armour, tunics that belonged to the Royal family, penny farthing bicycles to vacuum cleaners, women's fashion from the 19th century and even tickets to the Nuremberg war crimes trials. All the exhibits in the museum look at historical processes, revolutionary events, and the people behind them. The exhibition offers not only the big stories but also small everyday experiences, you are immersed in the lives of everyday people.

The permanent exhibition is supplemented by temporary special exhibitions housed in the modern exhibition building. The spacious new building, with a foyer constructed of glass and steel and a striking staircase, was opened in 2003, and can also be accessed via the inner courtyard of the Zeughaus.

Museum of Natural History
Invalidenstrasse 43
www.naturkundemuseum-berlin.de
Daily 10am – 6pm

Opened in 1889 by Kaiser Wilhelm II, this museum takes you on a tour through our planet and the natural world.

Upon entering you are welcomed by a dinosaur who leads you on a tour of the dinosaur museum with interactive virtual reality exhibits about the former rulers of our planet, reawaken these formidable animals, bringing them to life before your eyes. The highlight is the world's largest dinosaur skeleton, a colossal 13 metre tall Brachiosaurus. Even more spectacular is Tristan Otto, a gigantic Tyrannosaurus Rex. In the special exhibition "Tristan - Berlin bares teeth", you encounter a 66 million-year-old and 12-metre long dinosaur skeleton, one of the best-preserved specimens in the world. The skull alone, with its fearsome teeth, measures 1.5 metres.

The other exhibition halls each focus on a different theme and particularly popular are the so-called 'wet collections'. These are housed in the East Wing, a state-of-the-art building that has been restored in 2010. A total of 276,000 glass jars filled with 81,880 litres of alcohol, line almost 13 kilometres of shelves in this dramatic space. Fish, spiders, crabs, amphibians and mammals are conserved here. Gaze at the fascinating and curious objects behind the glass. In the exhibition "Highlights of the Art of Preservation", you can get up close with animals such as Bobby the gorilla and Knut the polar bear. Thanks to the latest techniques and the artistic abilities of the preservationists, the objects seem to be alive still.

DDR Museum
Karl-Liebnecht-Strasse
10178 Berlin
www.ddr-museum.de
10am – 8pm Daily

The GDR museum is one of the newest and most visited in Berlin, attracting over half a million visitors each year. For good reason: it is the only museum that deals exclusively with life in the former German Democratic Republic. The permanent exhibition takes its motto 'history to touch and feel' quite literally: visitors enter a scale model of a typical GDR prefabricated high-rise estate and will need all their wits about them. Information and exhibits are stowed away and hidden in drawers, closets and behind doors, making this the most interactive museum in Berlin. The exhibits can be touched and used, the kitchen still has the cooking smells of way back when, and a trabi is available to take visitors on a virtual tour of the area. Many former East German residents bring their families to show what life was like all those decades ago.

Deutsches Technik Museum
Trebbiner Strasse 9
www.dtmb.de
Tuesday – Friday, 9am to 5.30pm
Weekends and Holidays, 10am to 6pm

Berlin's German Museum of Technology is one of the most popular museums in the city and provides great family entertainment. It is a hands-on, activity-oriented fun tour of the cultural history of technology located at the Anhalter freight station, one of Berlin's former rail depots. The developments in transport, communication and energy technologies are presented in a total of 14 sections. On display are locomotives and planes, looms, jewellery, production and machine tools, computers, radios and cameras, diesel engines, steam engines, scientific instruments, paper machines, printing presses and much more.

The new Aeronautics and Space Collection opened in spring 2005, "why is the sky blue?" this and many other questions are answered in the Science Centre. Over 250 experiments illustrating phenomena of acoustics, optics, electricity, radioactivity and more demonstrate the fundamentals of science and technology.

The pendulum in the entrance building is living proof to all visitors that the earth rotates. Some of the other highlights include a hall of vintage locomotives, a reconstruction of the world's first computer from 1938, Konrad Zuse's Z1 a new aviation wing covering 200 years of German flight adventure from Hot Air Balloons to the Berlin Airlift. Film enthusiasts can find early film projectors while the Manufacturing Technology Department exhibits the transmission belt driven machinery and an example of the first mass-produced products such as the 1920s suitcase.

Berlin Philharmonic Hall
Herbert-von-Karajan-Strasse 1
www.berlin-philharmoniker.de

Founded in 1882, the Berlin Philharmonic is one of the most famous orchestras in the world. Famous conductors such as Herbert von Karajan and Wilhelm Furtwängler have shaped the history of the orchestra, which is currently under the baton of Sir Simon Rattle. The Berlin Philharmonic Hall, built in 1963 by architect Hans Scharoun, is a masterpiece of concert hall design. The auditorium offers excellent acoustics and splendid views from all seats because the orchestra sits in the middle. From the outside as well, the tent-like building is a sight to behold.

Top Tip:

Free lunchtime concerts, lasting between 30 and 40 minutes, are held in the foyer on Tuesdays at 1pm during the orchestra season. Check website for details.

East Side Gallery
Mühlenstrasse (near Oberbaumbrücke)

The East Side Gallery is a 1.3-kilometre-long painted stretch of the former Berlin Wall along the Mühlenstrasse in former East Berlin. It is the largest open-air gallery in the world with over one hundred original mural paintings. Inspired by the extraordinary events that were changing the world, artists from all around the globe rushed to Berlin after the fall of the Wall, leaving a visual testimony of the joy and spirit of liberation, which erupted at the time.

Wall murals had previously been a highlight for visitors and a Berlin attraction for years but were only to be found on the western side of the Wall.

Some of the best-known paintings such as "The Mortal Kiss" by Dimitrji Vrubel, of Erich Honecker and Leonid Brezhnev's mouth-to-mouth embrace and Birgit Kinder's Trabi (Trabant) knocking down the Wall. They have provided popular postcard material to this day. The paintings that still reflect the patchwork, eclectic and bohemian atmosphere of Berlin today, are a mixed bag of surreal images, political statements and graffiti-like effusions stretching from the Oberbaumbrücke to the Ostbahnhof.

The murals are under heritage protection. Restoration of over a quarter of the paintings that have suffered decay caused by defacement, weather and air pollution is underway.

Mach Mit for Kids
Senefelder Strasse 5
www.machmitmuseum.de
Tuesday – Sunday, 10am to 6pm

The MachMit! Museum is a very special place: in a converted church, children from four to twelve can discover, try things out and explore. Here, participation is explicitly and highly encouraged. In the centre of the exhibition space, in the main aisle and tower of the former Eliaskirche, is a large climbing frame made from wood.

Thematic experiential exhibitions, a historical soap shop, the house of mirrors, a museum printing shop make the museum visit here to an experience for all the senses. A stage with seats and the family café round out the exhibition experience for all the family.

Labyrinth Kinder Museum
Osloer Strasse 12
www.labyrinth-kindermuseum.de
Friday and Saturday, 1pm to 6pm
Sunday 11am, to 6pm
Extended hours during school holidays

The "Labyrinth Kindermuseum" is one of the leading children's museums within Germany, children from ages three to twelve can experience rotating participative exhibitions. Whether on subject fairy-tales, children's rights, health, world culture or others, touching, trying things out, playing and having fun is allowed here!

The interactive exhibitions aim to encourage the joy of learning and thereby inspire children to discover the world for themselves with all their senses. Learning takes place here "by doing" - by example, curiosity and active experience.

Top Tip: while running around the museum at heart's desire, balancing and trying things out are allowed; all visitors take off their shoes at the entrance, so don't forget treaded socks, slippers or plimsolls.

And here is one of the more unusual:

Deutsches Currywurst Museum
Schuetzenstrasse 70
www.currywurstmuseum.de
10am to 10pm Daily

The currywurst (curried sausage) is as much a part of Berlin as the Brandenburger Tor; it is the culinary emblem of Germany's capital city.

No German national dish inspires as many stories, preferences and celebrity connoisseurs as this one does; it is traditional and unconventional at the same time. Deutsches Currywurst Museum in Berlin is dedicated to the curried sausage, its friends and fans, the legends and stories coming along with it: in a unique exhibition designed as a special event. Tickets include a free tasting.

Streets and Squares

Nikolaiviertel

The Nikolai quarter or Nikolaiviertel is the oldest residential area of Berlin and considered by many to be the city's birthplace. With its mediaeval lanes and numerous restaurants and bars, it is one of the favourite destinations for visitors to Berlin.

In the Middle Ages, a trade route passed through this area and artisans and merchants settled at the junction of river and road. Around 1200, the St. Nicholas church, the oldest building in Berlin was built by craftsmen and fishermen around a settlement with two main areas: Berlin, which was a somewhat larger settlement locate east of the river Spree and Cölln, which was situated directly across from Berlin on the western banks.

Until the Second World War, the district was characterised by inns, stores, farms and small businesses. Artists such as Kleist, Hauptmann, Ibsen, Casanova, Strindberg or Lessing either lived or stayed here. The area, however, was largely destroyed by bombing in 1944 and for a long time it remained in ruins.

It was only in the early 1980's, in the run-up to the 750th anniversary of Berlin, that reconstruction work began. The architect Günter Stahn rebuilt the landscape of ruins based on historical models, the houses and streets were recreated as accurately as possible, so that the illusion exists that you are visiting old Berlin.

The main attractions, in addition to the St. Nicholas church, include the Ephraim Palace, a masterpiece of palace architecture of the 18th century Berlin. Equally beautiful is the Baroque style Knoblauch house built in 1760, which offers insight into world of the upper middle-class world through its rooms and valuable furniture.

When walking around the Nikolaiviertel you can't miss the bronze sculpture of St. George and the Dragon which decorates one of the area's small squares.

For a break from the bustle of the city just feet away or just a pleasant evening out, the Nikolaiviertel has more than 20 restaurants, cafés and pubs, many of them with local dishes and the typical Berlin atmosphere.

Alexanderplatz
Ranked a German National Tourist Board "Top 100 Sights in Germany"

'Alex' to Berliners, Alexanderplatz is the square named to honour Alexander I, Tsar of Russia, on his visit to Berlin in 1805. A cattle market in the Middle Ages, then a military parade square and an exercise ground for nearby barracks until the mid-19th century. In more recent times, one million people congregated here, on 4 November 1989 to demonstrate against the GDR regime shortly before the fall of the Berlin Wall. This was the largest anti-government demonstration in its history.

The transformation of Alexanderplatz into a modern transit junction and shopping area came about during the second half of the 19th century with developments such as the construction of the S-Bahn, Berlin's surface rail network in 1882 and the underground railway from 1913.

The square suffered heavy bombing during the war and gradually developed into a pedestrian zone during the 1960s, becoming a popular if rather shapeless urban area. Many of the well-known buildings, examples of East Berlin's attempt to compete with the West, were erected during this time. The Hotel Stadt Berlin, the Haus des Lehrers (Teachers' House), The House of Travel (with a slightly amusing ring to it given the notorious travel restrictions during the GDR) and the publishing house building - today's Berliner Verlag, offices of the Berlin daily paper, Berliner Zeitung.

Amongst the sights to look out for here is the TV tower, The Brunnen der Völkerfreundschaft (Fountain of Friendship amongst Peoples) and the landmark World Time Clock erected in 1969 which serves as a popular meeting place

Potsdamer Platz
Ranked a German National Tourist Board "Top 100 Sights in Germany"

Berlin's Potsdamer Platz, although not really a square, is the most striking example of the urban renewal that turned Berlin into the 'New Berlin' in the 1990s.

The square gets its name from the Potsdamer Tor, the city gate that stood on the main road from Berlin to Potsdam in the 18th century. In the early 20th century, the area was bustling with life and roaring traffic. In 1924, the first traffic lights in continental Europe were installed to guide the buses, trams, coaches and cars. The cultural and social elite met in the cafés and restaurants around the square.

The end of the second world war left the area devastated. It was at this point that the British, Soviet and American sectors met, it was divided by a wall and left as wasteland for 40 years.

The long debates about the future of Potsdamer Platz after the Cold War needed to resolve the issue of bringing authentic metropolitan life into an area which had been dead for years, integrating residential accommodation with shopping, leisure and business needs. However, after the two major investors DaimlerChrysler and Sony spent several years on spectacular mass construction projects, this has become the new heart of Berlin. The area today consists of the three developments known as Daimler City (1998), the Sony Centre (2000) and the Beisheim Centre (2004), which completely transformed the dormant wasteland where the Berlin Wall stood between east and West Berlin until 1989.

What can be seen today is believed to have resulted in a successful compromise - a mixture of the American plaza feel at the Sony Centre and a tree-lined European downtown around the Marlene Dietrich Platz producing a lively, buzzing atmosphere. And for a touch of glamour the prestigious Berlin International Film Festival, Berlin's most glamorous calendar event, held in February every year, moved its headquarters here in 2000. The red carpet is rolled out every February for A-list stars outside the Berlinale Palast, where stars and public mingle on the new Marlene Dietrich Platz.

The Panorama Punkt, with an observation deck 93m high, is reached by elevator for the best all-round view of the area in the brown-brick Kollhoff building.

The main attractions to be seen while walking around the Potsdamer Platz area include: Debis Tower and the DaimlerChrysler Atrium with its public spaces that include changing art exhibitions and the artificial water basin. The unmistakable symbol of the Sony Centre is an enormous white marquee-shaped roof covering the plaza of the centre that consists of six buildings. At night, this spectacular roof construction of steel, glass and fabric is lit up with a kaleidoscope of colour designed to reflect the changing nuances between sunset and complete darkness.

A few historical remains such as Lindenallee, Alte Potsdamer Strasse and Weinhaus Huth dating from 1910 enable you to occasionally forget the fact that this is a completely newly built area.

Bebelplatz

Built in 1740, Bebelplatz, formerly known as Kaiser Franz Joseph Platz, takes its name from August Bebel, co-founder of the Social Democratic Party (SPD). This square near the Royal Palace on Unter den Linden, formed part of Friedrich the Greats visionary project, as "Forum Fridericianum" it drew inspiration from the classical design of ancient Rome and was intended as a centre for intellectual and artistic endeavour. The Forum's buildings included the Alte Königliche Bibliothek (Old Royal Library), the Staatsoper (Opera House) erected 1741-42 and St Hedwig's Cathedral. It was the cost of wars being fought at the time that prevented the project from being completed.

Ironically, the square is better remembered today as the venue for the Nazi's first official book burning bonfire in May 1933, just opposite the Humboldt University. The action meant as a dire warning to Nazi opponents was instigated with the purposes of destroying the "Jewish mind and the whole rotten liberalist tendency". Over 20,000 works including those of the so-called subversive writers including Karl Marx, Berthold Brecht and Thomas Mann were set alight and destroyed. The "Versunkene Bibliothek" (sunken library), an underground library with empty shelves, serves as a symbolic reminder of the event.

Hackesche Höfe

Berlin's Hackesche Höfe (Hof means courtyard) is a historical area consisting of eight connecting, restored courtyards accessible through the main arched entrance on Rosenthalerstrasse.

The restoration of this heritage building completed in 1997, was a central factor in the emergence of one of Berlin's liveliest quarters since reunification. Since the 1990s the area around Hackesche Höfe has been synonymous with the vibrant urban renewal of the New Berlin, combining a mix of business and offices, residential housing, entertainment venues, art galleries, boutiques, bars and restaurants - the unmissable urban mix of the New Berlin which emerged in the 1990s. The area, also known as the Scheunenviertel, is one of Berlin's top entertainment hubs, popular with Berliners and visitors alike and a magnet for club-goers.

Historically, development of the Höfe went hand in hand with the growth of Berlin as a thriving urban centre. The expansion began around 1700, from an outer suburb known as Spandauer Vorstadt, located outside the Spandau City gate, Friedrich Wilhelm I built a new city wall and the former suburb became a new urban district belonging to Berlin. The area already had its own church, the Sophienkirche, from as early as 1712.

The influx of Jewish migrants and the exiled French Huguenots gave the district the cosmopolitan diversity that it has never lost. The first and largest synagogue in Germany was built in nearby Oranienburger Strasse in 1866 and the first Jewish cemetery established on the Grosse Hamburger Strasse, was destroyed by the Gestapo in 1943. Only one memorial tombstone, that of Jewish enlightenment philosopher Moses Mendelssohn, symbolically remains on the grounds.

The main attractions are the Chamäleon Variety Theatre housed in the original wine tavern and an original ceiling from one of the banqueting rooms in the large Hackescher Hof Restaurant, immediately to the left of the entrance.

Gendarmenmarkt
Ranked in the German Tourist Board "Top 100 Sights in Germany"

The Gendarmenmarkt is considered by many to be Berlin's most magnificent square. It is best known for the architectural trio composed of the Deutscher Dom, the Französischer Dom and Konzerthaus that together form one of the most stunning ensembles in Berlin. The 'domes' refer to the domed tower structures erected in 1785 by architect Carl von Gontard and were mainly intended to add stature and grandeur to the two buildings.

The square dates to 1700, part of King Friedrick I's plan for Friedrickstadt, an emerging new quarter of Berlin, where the recently expelled French Protestants or Huguenots had settled following the Edict of Potsdam in 1685 which granted them asylum in the Prussian capital.

After a full restoration completed in 1994, the French Church (Französischer Dom) now houses the Huguenot museum. In the Deutsche Dom rebuilt in the 1980s and restored in 1996, it is possible to visit a permanent exhibition on the history of the German Parliament called "Questions of German History". The statue of Friedrich Schiller located in the square's centre in 1871 was another victim of the Nazis purges, it was later returned to East Berlin in 1988 after a long exile in the western half of the city.

Gendarmenmarkt is also a great place to wander around and soak in the atmosphere, now part of re-built Mitte; it has become a lively urban space with its frequent performances at the concert hall. A bustling Christmas market and ice rink opens for the entire festive season from the first of Advent to the New Year. Some of Berlin's most glamorous hotels and restaurants are in this part of town.

Palaces

Schönhausen Palace
Tschaikowskystrasse 1
www.spsg.de
April – September, Tuesday to Sunday 10am to 6pm
October – March, Weekends 10am to 5pm

Built in the 17th century, Schloss Schönhausen has had a turbulent history; it is among the few castles in Berlin, which came through the Second World War undamaged.

It was here, Elector Frederick III, strategically plotted his installation of becoming the first King of Prussia 1701. In 1740, Frederick II gave this estate to his wife Elisabeth Christine, who lived there until her death in 1797. Worthy of special mention are the existing room decors of the late 17th century and 18th century, among them, a gorgeous stucco ballroom and the double staircase that stretches over three floors.

Wilhelm Pieck, the first president of the GDR, had his official residence here and it became the GDR government's official guesthouse in 1964. The guest apartment with its dressing room, bedrooms and bathrooms has largely retained its original condition. The decor is in strong colours and ultra-modern style as a demonstration of the GDR's progressiveness. International visitors such as Indira Gandhi, Fidel Castro and Mikhail Gorbachev slept here.

The same rooms were later used for the "round table" meetings during the regime change in 1990, and afterwards the Allied Forces held their "Two Plus Four" discussions here to decide the terms of the German Reunification.

After a long period of renovation, it was finally opened to the public again at the end of 2009 and now offers visitors a host of contrasts and new departures – a tour of three centuries of German history.

The exhibition on the ground floor focuses on Queen Elisabeth Christine. The wife of Frederick the Great used the palace in the 18th century for a long time as her summer residence. Her rooms have been restored to their original splendour: the chairs, mirrors, paintings and even wall coverings are all back where they used to be.

Babelsberg Palace
Im Park Babelsberg
www.spsg.de
April – October, Tuesday to Sunday 10am to 6pm

Prince Wilhelm, later Kaiser Wilhelm I, built Babelsberg Palace in 1833 and was the summer residence for over 50 years. Designed by architect Karl Friedrich Schinkel it is a pretty building in the English Tudor style with embattled walls, flanking towers and lancet windows. Terraces with mosaics, sculptures, beautifully arranged flowerbeds and a gothic fountain surround the palace. The English-style landscaped gardens and winding paths lead to Flatowturm tower, which was built between 1853 and 1856 from where the views of the Havel River are breath-taking, the water glitters in the sun; steamers glide by and, in the distance, is Glienicke Bridge.

Cecilienhof Palace
Im Neuen Garten
www.spsg.de
April – October, Tuesday to Sunday 10am to 6pm
November to March 10am to 5pm

In 1786 Friedrich Wilhelm II had the New Garden built between the Heiliger See and Jungfernsee lakes in the north of Potsdam: with its Marble Palace, shell grotto, an orangery with an Egyptian gateway, an icehouse in the shape of a pyramid and a palace kitchen in the style of a half-sunken Greek temple. Wörlitz Park had met its match. Thirty years later, after the death of Friedrich, the landscape gardener Peter Joseph Lenné came to Potsdam, still a gardening assistant, he began transforming the overgrown park. He created an English-style country park with broad paths, expansive lawns and sweeping vistas of Peacock Island, Glienicke Palace and Babelsberg Palace.

Some 100 years later, between 1914 and 1917, Kaiser Wilhelm II had Schloss

Cecilienhof built in the north of the gardens for his son Wilhelm and his wife Cecilie. The use of traditional building materials such as brick and wood help the house to blend in with its surroundings. The actual size of Schloss Cecilienhof only becomes evident upon closer inspection: the house has a total of 176 rooms, some of which were used by the Allies in 1945 for their Potsdam Conference. The centre of the building is formed by the great hall living area, which branches off into the official rooms of the royal couple. The rooms of the manor were divided into private spaces. The area for the head of the household included a smoking salon, a library and a breakfast room. The area for the lady of the house included a music salon, a study, and a small chamber designed in the style of a ship's cabin. A massive staircase of carved wood leads from here to the upper floor.

Glienicke Palace
Königsstrasse 36
www.spsg.de
April – October, Tuesday to Sunday 10am to 6pm
November to March 10am to 5pm

When young prince Carl of Prussia, then 21, returned to Berlin from his travels around Italy in 1823, he had only one dream: he wanted to live in an Italian villa set in a Mediterranean-style landscape. He loved Italy and it was to be here, on the Glienicke estate in the heart of Brandenburg's sandy plains, that he would build his dream home.

Architect Karl Friedrich Schinkel turned the original manor house into a summer residence, in a classical style, with clear outlines, well balanced and proportioned. Everywhere you go, you can see Italian-style elements such as the great fountain with the golden lion, which is modelled on the one found at the Villa Medici in Rome.

Glienicke Park was also lovingly designed. It is decorated with a variety of small buildings full of fanciful details, for instance, ancient mosaics from Carthage laid in the "Small Curiosity" tea pavilion. Schinkel also designed the terrace of the casino so that it offers a wonderful view of the River Havel.

Glienicke Bridge, which crosses the river directly behind the palace linking Berlin and Potsdam, can also be seen from here. During the Cold War, half of the bridge belonged to West Berlin and the other half belonged to the East. It became famous around the world as the place where spies were exchanged.

Köpenick
Schlossinsel 1
www.smb.museum
Tuesday to Sunday 10am to 6pm

A baroque style moated palace set on a small island, surrounded by an English-style park with elms and ginkgo trees, some of which are more than 350 years old, Köpenick Palace is simply steeped in history. Archaeologists have found the remains of graves from the Stone Age and Slavic fortifications from the 8th century on the site. In 1730 Friedrich

Wilhelm tried his own son by court-martial in the Heraldic Hall of the palace. Today, this is just one of the many rooms that have been lovingly restored. The palace also houses a branch of Berlin's arts and crafts museum.

Pfaueninsel and Palace
Nikolskoerweg
www.spsg.de
Only guided tours of the Palace are available
Please check website for opening times as the ferryboat, grounds and Palace all operate different schedules.

Pfaueninsel (Peacock Island) located on the Havel River in the southwest of Berlin. One and a half kilometres long and half a kilometre wide, the island can only be reached by ferry and was turned into a nature conservation area in 1924, as you walk around, you will see several free-roaming peacocks.

The white palace on Peacock Island was built by Friedrich Wilhelm II in 1794-97 and can be seen from quite a distance. It was designed as the crowning centrepiece at the end of a sweeping vista in the New Garden, as well as a place for the king to relax after his boat trips and spend the night with his beloved Wilhelmine Encke. The palace is characterised by its two circular towers, which are linked by a wrought-iron bridge to create the illusion of a medieval castle.

There are several other buildings set in the stunning landscaped gardens of Peacock Island; the Luise temple, the ruins of Meierei Abbey and the neo-gothic Kavaliershaus. The latter was used in the 1960s as the setting for several films.

As well as the peacocks walking around and showing off their colourful feathers, you can also watch woodpeckers and cormorants in Pfaueninsel park. In summer, the island is also home to four water buffaloes that help gardeners to mow the wetland. Archaeological finds reveal that Peacock Island has been inhabited for around 2,500 years.

Parks, Gardens and Recreation

Tiergarten

What Central Park is to New Yorkers, Hyde Park to Londoners and the Englischer Garten is to Munich, the same holds true in regard with the Tiergarten - the green lung of Berlin. Located in the city centre, next to attractions such as the Brandenburg Gate, it is even larger than the 210 hectares of Hyde Park.

Elector Friedrich III created the Tiergarten at the end of the 17th century from a former hunting preserve, as a "pleasure park for the people." Over the course of time, the park was redesigned several times, including a plan created by the famous landscape architect Peter Joseph Lenné who transformed Tiergarten between 1833 and 1838 into an English style park.

People come here for a stroll or having a family picnic, throwing a barbecue, playing ball games or just relaxing away from the bustle of the nearby city centre. Every Sunday in the summer, you can listen to the bells of the carillon; the 42-metre-high tower with its 68 bells is the fourth largest carillon in the world. A large playground or Spielplatz is located on the south-eastern corner near Potsdamer Platz. During wintertime it is even possible to sometimes skate on the small lakes inside the park if weather conditions allow.

Other popular attractions within the park are the Café am Neuen See, this small lake can freeze up in winter and provides a wonderful northern winter landscape and in the summer, it is transformed into a popular outdoor Self-Service Restaurant and Biergarten. Other well-liked areas include a very peaceful spot called Rousseau Island, and the English Gardens and coffee shop.

Grunewald Forest
In the times of the Berlin Wall, the Grunewald was the largest forested area in the western part of the city, and popular with walkers and cyclists. Today, it has become much quieter in the "Green Forest" but it is still beautiful, where all year round it is a relaxing place for walks. To the west, the Havel forms the forest boundary. To the south, via the ferry, visitors can cross over to the small Lindwerder Island, or climb up the Karlsberg and from the Grunewald Türm enjoy a wonderful view over the Havel and Wannsee. From the Teufelsberg, which is situated at the northern edge of the Grunewald, you have a magnificent view over the Grunewald and the surrounding areas. The Müggelberg, at 115 metres, is the highest elevation in Berlin. In winter, the mountain is used as a ski-slope and toboggan run, at all other times of the year, hang-gliders fly in the sky here.

Gardens of the World
Eisenacher Strasse 99
www.gaerten-der-welt.de
March & October 9am – 6pm Daily
November to February 9am to 4pm Daily
April to September 9am to 8pm Daily

The park at Marzahn began with the 1987 horticultural show "Berliner Gartenschau" and presents garden art from around the world. Nine exotic garden worlds were designed and built by architects and craftsmen from the respective countries using original materials.

The Chinese "Garden of the Reclaimed Moon", is the largest Chinese Garden in Europe. It was developed in very close cooperation with Berlin's twin city of Peking. A self-enclosed garden world with a pavilion, ponds, waterscapes, a Zen garden and impressive ornamental rocks, has been enchanting visitors to the Park since 2003. The Japanese "Garden of Merging Water" features typical Japanese plants such as Japanese maple, Japanese flowering dogwoods and Japanese lavender heather. Protected in a glasshouse, the Balinese "Garden of the Three Harmonies" presents a section of a traditional Balinese housing complex surrounded by tropical flora.

The Oriental "Garden of the Four Streams" represents the garden traditions of several oriental countries. The Korean "Seoul Garden" was a gift from the city of Seoul to Berlin. It occupies an area of 4,000 square metres and boasts a diverse naturalistic landscape, courtyards, elaborate decorative figures and a pavilion.

Serving as examples of European garden art, a Hampton Court-style maze and a labyrinth, like the one at Chartres Cathedral in France, were opened in 2007. The maze, consisting of yew hedges taller than the height of a person, is sited next to a paved labyrinth, giving visitors the opportunity to discover the differences between these two forms.

The Italian Renaissance Garden feature box tree topiary, artfully laid out paths, stone benches, statues and numerous potted plants in terracotta containers and conveys to the visitors the unique magic of Tuscany's famous villa gardens. In April 2011, the Christian Garden was opened. Its design concept is based on that of the cloister garden.

Karl Foerster was a shrub grower and garden philosopher from Potsdam-Bornim in the early 20th century, and the Karl Foerster Perennial Garden is a place of beauty and reconciliation with nature in keeping with his ideas.

The Weisser See

If the weather permits, it is worth taking a trip to the Weisser See (White Lake) and its jet fountain. The Weisser See is traditionally a popular swimming destination for many Berliners taking advantage of the clear water, palm trees and barbecue areas. It is also a lovely place to take a walk along the 1.3 kilometre path around the lake that leads to a small wildlife enclosure, numerous sculptures, and the Milchhaüschen restaurant.

To the west of the Weisser See, you will a find a place where few visitors venture. Here you can get a taste of the suburbs with old two-storey houses and craftwork houses that originate from old Berlin. Nearby on Behaimstrasse is the Neo-Romanesque church of St.-Joseph-Kirche. The Dutch Quarter built between 1925 and 1929 in the area around Schönstrasse and Woelckpromenade is worth a look. The red brick houses with the typical gables are a remarkable example of reformist housing and are considered forerunners to modern architecture.

On the other side of the Weisser See, there is a group of houses on Buschallee designed by Bruno Taut in 1925. The facades were restored in 1993 in light ochre and dark red while the rear of the buildings are white and pink.

Tegeler See and Forest

To the north of the city is Berlin's second largest lake and considered one of the most beautiful: the Tegeler See. The Tegeler See, with its seven islands, is a truly idyllic place: for taking walks, steamboat rides, sailing, surfing or bathing in the lido at the West bank. In the northern part of the lake, only a couple minutes away from Tegel-Ort, stands Berlin's oldest oak, the around 900-year-old "Fat Marie".

Berlin for Children

In earlier chapters I have already mentioned the two museums that are focused towards the family and the zoo – a top attraction for all. Here are some more attractions that are good for families.

AquaDom and Sealife Berlin
Spandauer Strasse 3
Mon – Fri 9am to 6pm
Saturday 10am to 6pm

Just a short walk from Alexanderplatz, you can take an exciting underwater trip and discover more than 5,000 fascinating aquatic animals. Follow the path that water takes from the Spree River to the depths of the Atlantic and then on to tropical areas. Experience a very special type of dive in the AquaDom, the largest freestanding aquarium in the world. Get in the glass elevator and swim through one million litres of saltwater and swarms of tropical fish.

Berlin Dungeon
Spandauer Strasse 2
Daily 10am to 6pm

The Berlin Dungeon takes you through the horrible history of the city in around an hour. You travel from the Middle ages to the 19th century, different themed areas describe real events from history, treading the line between fun and horror. If you manage to escape the Black Death by floating down a raft on the river Spree, you will then meet the twisted Monk, the legendary White Lady or Berlin's infamous serial killer Carl Grossmann. All of the characters are played by real actors and the live shows are in both German and

English.

Forcki Adventure Play Area
Forckenbeckplatz
www.forcki.de
Monday – Wednesday 1pm to 6pm
Thursday & Friday 2pm to 7pm

A supervised adventure play area that spreads over 4000 square metres and a great place to run of some energy. Crocodiles, giant turtles and elephants spouting water – in between screaming children run riot in around the paddling pool, wet from head to toe but with broad smiles on their faces. There's a lot going on in the Forcki in Berlin Friedrichshain, particularly in summer; castles are built in the large sandpits and mud channels are dug. The children enjoy themselves on slides and swings, on the ropeway, exercise on the mini-climbing wall or climb on the tree house. There is also enough space for ball games and skateboarding.

Occasionally local groups offer projects and activities where children can join in: from cooking together through computer games up to dancing. The range for fathers with children is particularly popular. There is also a café for refreshments.

Snow White and the Seven Dwarfs Play Area
Mommsenstrasse 48

The playground in the Mommsenstrasse is called "Snow White and the Seven Dwarfs" and it will invite you to journey into fairy tale land with its lovingly designed wood figures. On the 2,500 square metre playground there is a dwarf house with a baby slide, a dwarf mine with lifts for sand buckets and a dwarf pump to really splash around. While the little ones sit in the baby swing the big ones can run through the Prince's castle, climb ladders and zoom down slides and climbing poles. For the older ones there are two table tennis tables, a basketball court and a football pitch next door.

There is another highlight for kids just ten minutes away: the Spielhaus (play house) Schillerstraße, a supervised playground with a colourful range of sport, play and creative and artistic work. The children can ride tricycles or drive a go-cart, walk on stilts, dance, play music, make things or use a computer here.

Pinke-Panke Children's Farm
Am Bürgerpark 15- 18
www.kinderbauernhof-pinke-panke.de
April to October; Tuesday to Friday 12pm to 6.30pm, Weekends 10am to 6.30pm
March to November; Tuesday to Friday 12pm to 5.30pm, Weekends 10am to 5.30pm

Opened in 1991, the farm is a place of adventure and play, for encounters and common projects, where ecological principles are at the forefront. By helping in the daily work on the farm, children and young people can experience the farm adventure up close and in doing so observe nature and get to know it in a really special way.

Sit around an open fire, cook and bake bread on a stick, make jewellery from soapstone and repair your bike in the workshop. You can also feed the more than 70 animals together with the farm staff.

The Pinke-Panke offers children, young people and adults an experience close to nature in the middle of the big city Berlin.

Planetarium and Observatory
Munsterdamm 90
www.wfs.be.schule.de
Opening Times and Programmes vary

This combination of public observatory and large planetarium is set on Insulaner hill in Berlin's Schöneberg district; it is an ideal place from which to explore planets and moons on a clear day. Whether it is raining or stormy, the planetarium opens its magnificent artificial night sky.

Founded in 1947, the Wilhelm-Foerster observatory is an astronomical centre of learning, looking at both classical and modern astronomy. At the Zeiss Planetarium, which opened in 1965, all the movements in the night sky can be demonstrated. Projectors are used to ensure that clouds are blended in, landscapes and panoramas are created, and shooting stars can be seen. In addition, the planetarium offers a wide-ranging programme regarding astronomy.

Suggested Tours

Here are details of 4 walking tours that allow you to see some of the sights (in **bold** type) of Berlin.

Mitte – Around Brandenburg Gate and Alexanderplatz
Approx. distance: 5.5km

Begin at the **Siegessäule** (Victory Column); walk through the beautiful **Tiergarten**

towards the **Brandenburg Gate**. To your left you have the **Reichstag** with its magnificent dome. As you pass through the Brandenburg Gate you enter **Pariser Platz** with the nearby embassies of the UK and USA and the world-renowned **Adlon Hotel**, where Michael Jackson famously dangled his baby from the window.

Proceed along one of Berlin's most famous streets, **Unter den Linden** and you can take a right turn along **Friedrichstrasse** and visit the **Gendarmenmarkt** and the luxury store, **Galeries Lafayette**. Return to Unter den Linden and you will pass the **Humboldt University, the State Opera House and Berlin Cathedral**. Here you cross Lustgarten Square to **Museum Island**. You should then cross over the Schlossbrücke Bridge on Unter den Linden and pass the **Rotes Rathaus**, carrying on to the **TV Tower** and **Alexanderplatz**. There are many shops, cafes and restaurants near Alexanderplatz.

If you want to visit the **Hackescher Markt** with its boutiques and cafes it is just a short walk along Dirckenstrasse.

Top Tip: You can cover the same area with the 100 bus from Zoo station to Alexanderplatz, with stops at the Siegessäule, Bellevue Palace and the Reichstag.

From Brandenburg Gate to Kurfürstendamm
Approx. distance 4km to the top of the Kurfürstendamm

Leaving the **Brandenburg Gate**, you will have the **Tiergarten** on your right as you walk along Ebertstrasse, along past the **Memorial to the Murdered Jews**. Ahead of you, the skyscrapers of **Potsdamer Platz** will already be visible. On arrival you will see the Sony Centre, the DaimlerChrysler Quarter and as you cross Potsdamer Platz you will reach the **Cultural Forum, the Philharmonic Hall, the Berlin State Library** and the **New National Gallery**.

From here you have 2 options; you can either walk along Reitpietschufer, then Von-der-Heydt-Strasse and Corneliusstrasse passing through Berlin's Embassy quarter, ending at Budapesterstrasse, which will lead you to the **Kaiser Wilhelm Memorial Church**. Alternatively, the M29 bus will take you on almost the same route.

You have now completed the walk at the top of **the Kurfürstendamm**; you can take a stroll through it shops and cafes and visit **Tauentzienstrasse** and the famous **KaDeWe**.

If you would like to visit **Charlottenburg Palace**, the bus 109 will take you along the Kurfürstendamm to the palace. Afterwards you can take the M45 bus to **Savignyplatz**, a traditional quarter and enjoy a glass of wine or beer.

Around Friedrichshain-Kreuzberg
Approx. distance 9km (although some of this can be done by UBahn)

Take a tour of one of Berlin's most hip and happening districts; this tour is not so much about the sights but the atmosphere.

Start at **Bergmannstrasse**; look at the second-hand shops and cafes. Locals enjoy taking a stroll around the **Urban Inland Harbour**, with its summer Mediterranean atmosphere. A short distance from here is the **Turkish Market** on Maybachufer, with an array of exotic fruits and vegetables, spices and fabrics.

A short walk from here, but an all-together different atmosphere is the cool and chic area of **Oranienstrasse**. From here you can either walk up to **Oranienplatz** or take the oldest underground line, U1, to Schesischer Tor and the **Wrangel neighbourhood**. Here you can sip refreshments overlooking the Spree River.

Cross over the **Oberbaumbrücke** to the student district around **Simon-Dach-Strasse**. Here there are numerous lively bars, cafes and restaurants that come to life at sunset. Relax in the evening in one of the restaurants around **Boxhagener Platz**.

Top Tip: The BiOriental Turkish Market is on Tuesday and Fridays 11am to 6pm and the Neukölln fabrics market on Saturdays 11am to 5pm.

Museum Island

This tour will allow you to visit 5 museums in one day and see the best the Island has to offer.

Firstly, the **Altes Museum** and the antiquities of classical Greece and Rome. The Treasure Chamber on the ground floor contains delicate jewellery and close by is the expressive sculpture of Doryphoros (Spear Bearer) by Polycleitus.

Next the **Neues Museum** and in this recently refurbished museum you can see the fantastic Ancient Egyptian works of art – the Bust of Nefertiti.

Then to the **Alte Nationalgalerie** and its collection of 19th century masterpieces, the most famous being "Monk by the Sea" by Friedrichs. Another highlight is the sculpture of the two princesses showing the later Queen Louise and her sister.

The largest museum is the **Pergamon**, which takes you on a fantastic journey through the ancient world with monumental reconstructions.

Finally, is the **Bode-Museum**; its grand interior is a fantastic setting for the collection of Byzantine Art, mosaics and sculptures.

Top Tip: don't forget your Berlin Card that allows you free entry to these museums.

Berlin to Potsdam

Berlin's outer districts also have a lot to offer and here you will take in lakes, parks, palaces and stadiums.

Take the train from the city centre to the **Olympic Stadium**, built for the 1936 Olympic Games and still used today for regular sporting events. Although refurbished, many of the original features remain.

From here take the classic double-decker bus 218 to **Grunewald Türm Tower** in the **Grünwalder forest**. Climb the 204 steps to get breathtaking views of the forest and the River Havel. Get back on the bus **to Pfaueninsel** (Peacock Island); it is only a short ferry crossing to the Island, its peacocks and small palace that dates to 1794.

Return to the bus and back to Wannsee station, passing the shores **of Lake Wannsee**, here you board the S-Bahn to Potsdam Main Station. In **Potsdam** wander round the streets, shops, cafes and restaurants and the alleyways of the Dutch quarter. A visit to **Sanssouci Palace** should not be missed and just a short walk from the centre. This was the summer residence of Frederick the Great and is a beautiful palace set in fantastic gardens. Ranked in the German Tourist Board "Top 100 Sights in Germany"

You can return to the city by train.

Top Tip: The 218 bus leaves every 2 hours from Theodor-Heuss-Platz station for Peacock Island (11.15 am to 7.15pm)

Festivals and Events

Here is a list of festivals and events throughout the year, full details given where possible, but it is always recommended you check websites in case of change.

Internationale Grüne Woche Berlin
Messegelände am Funkturm
www.gruenewoche.de

10 days in January

A festival of food and drink from around Germany and the World. Here producers introduce new foods and drinks for tasting, there are live animals on display and many experts from the agriculture and horticulture fields for you to talk to.

Long Night of Museums
Various venues
www.lange-nacht-der-museen.de
Late January

Twice a year, around 100 of Berlin's museums, collections, archives and exhibition halls stay open into the early hours with special events, concerts, readings, lectures and performances for the 'Long Night of the Museums'. A ticket gets you free travel on special shuttle buses and regular public transport.

Six Day Berlin
Velodrome
Paul Heyse Strasse 26

Starting in 1909, the Berlin Six Day Race is the oldest six-day race in the world. In its first year, 15 teams of two cyclists each competed in the exhibition hall at Berlin Zoo for glory.
On six consecutive evenings several teams, each consisting of two racing cyclists, compete. There is a different race every night, with varying degrees of speed and stamina. The competitions include the traditional, international "pacemaker race", a derby and a sprint race. In all the competitions, champions from all over the world compete against amateurs.

Berlin International Film Festival
Potsdamer Platz
www.berlinale.de
Mid-February

Now approaching 60 years old, the Berlinale is one of the world's major cinema festivals, featuring over 300 movies from all five continents. It is located primarily at the Potsdamer Platz cinemas and attended by international stars, providing this normally glamour-proof city with a bit of glitz in the dead of winter.

Fasching
Mid-February (Shrove Tuesday is the final day)

This is Germany's answer to Mardi Gras, people where colourful costumes and take to the streets to party.

Spring Festival
Kurt-Schumacher-Damm 207
March

Starting the Berlin Festival season, the spring funfair has a great choice of amusements for all the family. Around 60 showmen offer funfair pleasure with rollercoasters, fun houses, a ghost train, Ferris wheels, and many more rides at the Zentraler Festplatz in Reinickendorf.
To satisfy your hunger there are half-metre bratwursts, crêpes, roasted almonds, candy floss and many more mouth-watering delights. A party tent offers a musical programme with shows by bands and solo artists. On two Saturdays during the festival the sky will light up at 10pm with a grand display of fireworks.

Festtage
Staatsoper
April

At Festtage Berlin international opera stars and the state orchestra "Staatskapelle Berlin" come together and turn the Staatsoper into a special venue with just the right atmosphere for classical music.

May Day Riots
Kreuzberg
1st May

This lively challenge to authority has taken place since 1987

German Open
LTTC Rot-Weiss, Grunewald
www.german-open.org
Early May

This is the 5th largest ladies tennis championship in the World and tickets can be hard to come by.

Karneval der Kulturen
Kreuzberg
www.karneval-berlin.de
4 days in May (including Whit Sunday)

Inspired by the London Notting Hill Carnival and intended as a celebration of Berlin's ethnic and cultural diversity, the long and popular weekend (always Pentecost) centres on a multi-cultural parade involving around 50 colourful floats, hundreds of musicians and thousands of spectators. The route changes every year, check the website.

International Museum Day
Various Locations
May

Every year since 1978 the worldwide community of museums has celebrated the International Museum Day. The event highlights the role of museums in enriching society, promoting cultural exchange and mutual understanding among peoples. In 2017, more than 35,000 museums participated in the event in about 145 countries.

Museuminselfestival
Museumsinsel and Kulturform
www.smb.museum
May to September

This festival features open- air events on Museumsinsel and near Potsdamer Platz such as rock and classical music, plays, readings and film showings.

Berlin Philharmonie at the Waldbühne
Waldbühne, Am Glockenturm, Charlottenburg
www.berlin-philharmonic.com
June

The Philharmonic ends its season with an open-air concert that sells out months in advance. Over 20,000 Berliners light the atmospheric 'forest theatre' with candles once darkness falls.

Open-Air Concerts
Monbijou Park

Every Monday through the summer, the Amphitheatre in Monbijou Park is transformed into a romantic concert stage. Surrounded by an enthusiastic audience, international artist's present music styles such as Argentinean tango, Portuguese fado, Italian chansons, or Balkan pop.

Citadel Music Festival
Spandau
www.citadel-music-festival.de
End of May to mid-August

With a unique flair the Citadel at Spandau located on the River Havel is one of the most beautiful open-air locations of Berlin and attracts thousands of music fans each year to hear the likes of Snow Patrol, Alanis Morissette, The Cranberries, Lynyrd Skynyrd.

Open Air Gallery
Oberbaumbrücke
June

Since its premiere in 2002, the Open-Air Gallery has been held twice every year. The Open-Air Gallery turns the Oberbaumbrücke into a mile of art with more than a hundred artists display their paintings, photographs and sculptures on the distinctive bridge between Kreuzberg and Friedrichshain.
The aim of the Open-Air Gallery is to stimulate the dialogue between artists and visitors. Even though the festival's popularity has grown over the years, it has maintained its original concept: Both professionals and young talents are given the chance to present their art in the categories paintings/graphics, sculptures and photography.

During the festival, visitors can get involved. A 120-metre-long canvas invites everyone to paint, draw or doodle.

Long Night of Sciences
Various Locations
Mid – June

From late afternoon to midnight over 70 scientific institutions across Berlin and Potsdam give an insight into their work, conduct exciting experiments and offer the latest research findings. There are more than 2000 events in research centres, institutes, laboratories and archives - from the natural sciences and engineering to politics and the humanities - that attract around 28,000 visitors every year.

A shuttle bus service along different routes makes it easy for participants to get from one venue to another. The service starts at 5 pm and ends at midnight and is free of charge for anyone who owns a ticket for the Long Night of the Sciences.

Fête de la Musique
Various venues throughout the city
www.fetedelamusique.de
21 June

Berlin celebrated its first Fête de la Musique in 1995 and has been organized by the Fête Company ever since. Having started as a small movement, the festival has since grown into one of the largest and most widely attended music festivals in Berlin.
On June 21st every year, you can listen to all styles of music all over Berlin for free. Bands, orchestras, choirs, soloists and DJs perform music on public squares, in the streets and in other public spaces, creating a fantastic atmosphere. In total, there are over one hundred venues - open-air and indoor - across the city, most of them in the inner-city districts of Friedrichshain- Kreuzberg, Mitte and Pankow.

The Fête de la musique is not a Berlin event as such, musicians from over 340 cities worldwide, celebrate the beginning of summer with the open-air music festival.

Berliner Volksfestsommer
Zentraler Festplatz am Kurt-Schumacher-Damm, Reinickendorf
www.volffest-berlin.de
4 weeks in June and July

Evolving from the popular German-French Fair, the "Berliner Volksfestsommer" promises a fun day out for friends, couples and families. There is lots of entertainment with about 150 performers, rides and rollercoasters, a ghost train, and the "Poseidon" water ride. The central food and party village tempts visitors with music and treats such as tarte flambé, Thuringian rostbratwurst and garlic baguette.

Every Saturday visitors can enjoy a fantastic fireworks display.

Bergmannstrasse Festival
Bergmannstrasse
www.bergmannstrassenkreuzbergjazzt.de
End June

Every year Kreuzberg's Bergmannstrasse, one of the most attractive and diverse areas in Berlin's old city centre, transforms into a must-see scene for jazz and music fans. "Kreuzberg jazzt" lasts for three days and showcases over 50 groups on a series of stages and has given the Bergmannstrasse event a reputation far beyond the city borders. The jazz festival combines Kreuzberg's characteristic lively atmosphere with stunning music, great food and a multicultural feel good factor irresistible for young and old.

Christopher Street Day Parade
www.csd-berlin.de
Late June / early July

Originally a gay parade organised to commemorate the 1969 riots outside the Stonewall Bar on Christopher Street in New York, the fun and flamboyant parade has become one of the summer's most enjoyable and inclusive street parties, attracting straights as well as gays

Berlin Lacht (Berlin Laughs)
Mariannenplatz and Alexanderplatz
www.berlin-lacht.de
June and July

An International street theatre festival that takes place in June at Mariannenplatz and in late July and early August at Alexanderplatz. In front of street scenery artists are presenting their performances: Professional artistry, clownery, acrobatics, pantomime, art installations, stilt theatre, puppetry, street music and fire performances for the whole family in public. Berlin Lacht! offers entertainment for everyone.

Classic Open Air
Gendarmenmarkt
www.classicopenair.de
4-7 days in early July

For almost 3 decades famous names open this concert series held in one of Berlin's most beautiful squares. Every summer since 1992, the Gendarmenmarkt, in the heart of Berlin, has been transformed into a spectacular backdrop for the Classic Open-Air Festival - a series of concerts that attracts crowds from the world over. Since its inception, the festival has attracted about 640,000 people to 112 concerts, with a musical range covering everything from opera and stage musicals, to pop classics, soul, swing and jazz.

Botanical Night
Botanical Gardens
Königin-Luise Strasse 6
July

The Botanical Garden in Zehlendorf district opened in 1910. Since then it has become one of the world's most famous botanical creations. The 43 hectares large area provides space for about 22,000 different plants from all over the world.

During the Botanical Night, which continues until around 2am, a 16-kilometre-long path along the flower beds and several themed gardens are illuminated and guides visitors to many attractions. Various mythical creatures appearing in between flowers turn the garden into a romantic and magical place. There is also a cultural programme with cabaret, theatre, dance performances and food delicacies. It is completed by a huge romantic firework above the Italian garden which paints flowers in the sky.

Deutsch-Amerikanisches Volksfest
Truman Plaza, Zehlendorf
www.deutsch-amerikanisches-volksfest.de
4 weeks in July and August

The German-American Folk Festival celebrates the American way of life with amusement rides, live music, food and drink. Originally established by the US forces stationed in West Berlin, the German-American Festival offers a popular mix of carnival rides, cowboys doing lasso tricks, candy floss, hot dogs and American beer. Each year around 100,000 visitors enjoy the exciting entertainment programme at Marienpark in Berlin-Mariendorf.

The Summer Festival of the Kurfürstendamm
Kurfürstendamm
www.agcity.de
August

From 3rd to 19th of August 2012, the most prestigious avenues worldwide including the Champs-Elysees, Regent Street and Bond Street, are celebrating the international festival "Summer in the City" with music, arts and crafts as well as culinary offers. At the Kurfürstendamm in Berlin visitors can find wine and cheese from Paris or fish & chips from London. Additionally, to the international delicacies, artists, musicians and a varied programme live on stage will bring the flair of the avenues from all over the world to Berlin.

Tanz im August
Hallesches Ufer 32, Kreuzberg
www.tanzimaugust.de
August

Tanz im August is Germany's leading modern dance festival and an annual showcase for global dance trends, with big-name participants and an international reputation. Dance in August is a well-established international contemporary dance festival that is open to and encourages new formats and innovative choreographies.

International Berlin Beer Festival
Karl MarxAllee
www.bierfestival-berlin.de
Early August

This beer festival has a 2.2 kilometre beer garden stretching from Frankfurter Tor to Strausberger Platz and is featured in the Guinness Book of World Records as the World's longest beer garden. You will find delicious food, good music as well as over 2000 beers.

Potsdam Palace Night
Potsdam
Mid-August

The Potsdam Palace Night makes the pompous lives of the Prussian kings come alive. For two days, the gardens, temples and palaces around Sanssouci Palace open their doors for visitors and allow them a glimpse into the baroque lifestyle of Frederick the Great and his royal contemporaries.
Throughout the gardens, visitors are greeted by musicians playing classical tunes. Dance

and theatre performances give visitors an insight into popular attractions from centuries ago, while several informal lectures acquaint inquiring minds with the thoughts and visions of the society of the 18th century.

Dressed up actors wearing costumes from an era long gone promenade between the Orangery and the New Palais, the Chinese Tea House and the Roman Baths all evening. The Potsdam Palace Night culminates in a firework display at midnight on both Friday and Saturday.

Long Night of Museums
Various venues
www.lange-nacht-der-museen.de
Late August
6pm – 2am

Twice a year, around 100 of Berlin's museums, collections, archives and exhibition halls stay open into the early hours with special events, concerts, readings, lectures and performances for the 'Long Night of the Museums'. A ticket gets you free travel on special shuttle buses and regular public transport.

Kreuzberger Festliche Tage
Viktoriapark, Kreuzberg
www.kreuzberger-festliche-tage.de
Late August, early September

This annual late summer festival in Viktoriapark offers music, games, beer and food.

Musikfest Berlin
Berliner Festspiele, Charlottenburg
www.berlinerfestspiele.de
Late August, early September

During the Musikfest, Berlin's concert halls resound with classical music performed by renowned national and international orchestras, choirs and chamber ensembles. The festival not only attracts hundreds of musicians but also thousands of fans of classical music from all over the world.

Over the course of the 19 festival days, almost 27 events featuring over 80 works by 40 composers, 20 orchestras, instrumental and vocal ensembles and countless soloists perform at various locations around the city.

Popkomm
Messe Berlin, Charlottenburg
www.popkomm.de
September

Europe's largest domestic music industry trade fair takes place over 3 days in September, as well as the trade-only conference, the city host's many live events for the public.

Heritage Day
Various Locations
September
www.tag-des-offnen-denkmals.de

The Heritage Day, known as "Day of the Open Monument" in Berlin, takes place every year in September and is a Europe-wide event. Its aim is to inform people of the meaning of cultural heritage and to awaken their interest for the care and preservation of ancient monuments.
At the "Day of the Open Monument" in Berlin, monument conservationists carry out guided tours on, at and in ancient monuments, buildings and places which normally are not accessible for visitors. While talking about but also showing their day-to-day work, the experts bring it to life for visitors and strengthen people's understanding of cultural sites. Other experts, such as archaeologists and craftsmen demonstrate certain work techniques and lead the visitors' eye to details which would normally remain hidden.

Berlin Marathon
www.berlin-marathon.com
Last Sunday in September

The Berlin marathon is one of the world's biggest marathons with around 60,000 entrants. It takes place over two days to accommodate runners, wheelchair athletes and in-line skaters. Because Berlin is flat and the weather moderate in September, world records are often challenged.

Oktoberfest
The World-famous beer festival takes place in Munich every year from mid-September to early October, but not to miss out Berlin can also offer you the experience in the city too:

Spreewiesn Oktoberfest at Postbahnhof
At the Spreewiesn, just a few steps away from Ostbahnhof station, there are beer glasses full of Löwenbräu Festbier, Obstler (fruit schnapps), Dirndl and Lederhosen. The guests can expect an original Bavarian band, half roast chicken and of course pork knuckles. The outdoor terrace is available for the warm evenings in autumn. Guests are kindly asked to dress according to the occasion. Dirndls, lederhosen, checked scarves, jackets and shirts are obligatory. At least a little effort and Bavarian joy of life should be recognizable on the evening.

Oktoberfest at Alexanderplatz
The centre of the Oktoberfest at Alexanderplatz is a large, atmospheric festival tent with authentic live music. There is also an open-air beer garden with over 1,000 seats and lots of Bavarian specialities such as pork knuckles, Breze, roast pork and chicken, and sweet treats. At a dirndl competition the most beautiful dirndl is chosen every evening.

Oktoberfest Berlin at Kurt-Schumacher-Damm
www.schaustellerverband-berlin.de
The Oktoberfest Berlin has been celebrated since 1949. The festival ground also provides

numerous fun activities for families such as bumper cars, merry-go-rounds and rides. The 85 x 25 metres large party tent, a brass band, typical Bavarian specialities such as pork knuckles, pretzels and roast chicken, and not least freshly brewed beer make sure that local fans of the Oktoberfest get that "Wiesn" feeling in Berlin.

Day of German Unity
3 October

The fall of the Berlin Wall on the 9th of November in 1989, which marked the end of the Cold War, paved the way for German reunification barely a year later. The Unification Treaty that was signed on the 20th of September in 1990 and declares the 3rd of October the national holiday, sealing the end of the division of Germany. The historical event of German reunification is celebrated with a three-day festival around Platz der Republik at Reichstag and Brandenburg Gate. In that area, various stages host live bands and stands sell food, drinks and sweets.

Festival of Lights
www.festival-of-lights.de
October

The Berlin Festival of Lights is one of the largest and best-known illumination festivals in the world. It takes place each year in October, where for 12 consecutive nights, Berlin's world-famous landmarks, cultural monuments, historical buildings, streets and other locations become transformed through light, projections and events.

Pyronale
Maifeld, near Olympic Stadium
October

On two nights in mid-October, around 60,000 spectators watch the gigantic fireworks in magnificent displays, and the most spectacular pyrotechnics in Germany. This exceptional event is not only a competition but also a fantastic occasion for spectators and is one of the main attractions in Berlin.

JazzFest Berlin
Berliner Festspiele, Charlottenburg
www.berlinerfestspiele.de
November

This 4-day festival features a wide spectrum of jazz from an array of internationally renowned artists, and a fixture in the event calendar since 1964. For over 50 years, jazz musicians from Berlin and all over the world have come together to play at the JazzFest, making the festival one of the oldest and most prestigious in Europe. Among its guests have been big names such as Miles Davis, Charles Mingus and Duke Ellington.

Berliner Märchentage
Various venues
www.berliner-maerchentage.de
Mid November

The Berlin Fairytale Festival lasts for around 3 weeks and celebrates tales from around the world each year, with some 400 storytelling and music events in a carnival atmosphere.

Worldtronics
Haus der Kulturen der Welt
www.hkw.de
November

A festival showcasing the world of electronic music, in a city that loves the music. Guest musicians come from all over, while the trade fair covers everything from books, clubs and labels to software and sound laboratories.

Christmas Markets

Many people like to visit the Christmas Markets in Germany and Berlin is no exception with over 60 around the city for you to wander through. The major Christmas markets begin in Berlin, as in the rest of Germany, in the last week of November and are open every day until Christmas Eve, with some open until the end of December.

220 trees in Unter den Linden will be lit up from mid-November until 31 December which will add to the festive atmosphere in the city.

The shops in Berlin will usually be open on the 2nd and 4th Sundays in Advent from 1pm until 6pm.

The Markets
www.weihnachteninberlin.de

There are markets throughout the city centre and surrounds, amongst others; there are markets on Alexanderplatz, in front of the Rotes Rathaus, by the Opernpalais on Unter den Linden, Potsdamer Platz and on Breitscheidplatz (around the Kaiser Wilhelm Gedächtniskirche). Those ones are all free to visit; there is also one in Gendarmenmarkt, which charges a small entry fee (1 euro). They generally stay open until well after the shops have closed, usually 9pm, so it can be a nice way to end the day, plus the atmosphere is just that bit more special (and the Glühwein seems that extra bit more warming) after dark.

Of course, there are many more all over the but hopefully this small selection will serve as an example of what you can find, also these are central which is good if you are only there for a few days and want to do some sightseeing as well.

Top Tip:
Please note that closing times will vary on Christmas Eve, most markets will close early around 2pm.

Gendarmenmarkt
11am – 10pm Daily
www.gendarmenmarktberlin.de

Berlin's most popular and favourite Christmas Market.

The Weihnachtszauber market in Gendarmenmarkt, unlike most markets, charges an entry fee (though still only 1 euro) which is donated to charity and some the things on offer are more expensive, but still worth a visit. The smells of roast almonds and chestnuts, warm Glühwein and hot chocolate fill this beautiful square. The 170 stalls are particularly good for arts and crafts. Jugglers, fire-eaters, choirs and classical, jazz or

Gospel ensembles provide a varied entertainment programme on each market day. It is within walking distance of the Opernpalais, so if you feel like doing a market crawl, you can go all the way from Alexanderplatz to Gendarmenmarkt and not be away from a Christmas market for more than about 5 minutes! It's open from November until December 31st as they also hold a New Year's Eve event there.

Wintertraum am Alexa
1.30pm – 10pm Monday to Thursday
Midday to 10.30pm Friday to Sunday

Wintertraum am Alexa (Winter Dream at Alexa), which stretches along Alexanderstrasse to Jannowitzbrücke, along the side of the Alexa shopping centre is the largest Christmas Market in Berlin and attracts around 2 million visitors. This large market has 150 stalls selling traditional gifts and decorations as well as rides such as a Ferris wheel and a small train for children. The market has increased in size in recent years and it has the advantage of being close to the shops around Alexanderplatz, which you might find worth visiting for Christmas shopping such as the department store Galeria Kaufhof.

A special feature of the market is the Christmas pyramid decorated with more than 5000 lights. It is the biggest walk-in Christmas pyramid in Europe. On the ground floor of the pyramid snacks are available and the platform on top offers nice views.

Rotes Rathaus
Midday – 10pm Daily

The market by the Rotes Rathaus, known as Berliner Weihnachtszeit, is of course also close to Alexanderplatz, so you can always visit the two, plus take a wander through the nearby Nikolaiviertel, which you might also find good for gifts.
Visitors to the Christmas market at Berlin Town Hall travel back into historic Berlin with street artists such as organ grinders and musicians, an Old Berlin setting and traditional stalls selling authentic arts and crafts. Performers present scenes of life in Berlin as it happened here one hundred years ago.

There are a lot of tasty treats waiting for the visitors, from the traditional mulled wine, or Glühwein, to roasted almonds, bratwursts, freshly baked bread and gingerbread. Look out for the stall of Kleinbrennerei Fitzke if you like spirits and liqueurs, it has for sale a huge array of different fruit brandies, liqueurs and spirits.
Santa Claus comes too: Three times a day he rides on his sleigh pulled by his reindeer around the market and is happy to pose for a photograph.

A 50-metre giant Ferris wheel provides an excellent view of the beautifully illuminated Berlin city centre. Historic carrousels offer delight both for children and adults. A special treat for the little ones is a trip on the train that enters a fantastic, snowy fairy-tale forest. Another popular highlight of this market is the ice rink where skaters skate around the impressive Neptune Fountain.

The Nostalgischer Weihnachtsmarkt
11.30am – 9pm Daily

The Nostalgischer Weihnachtsmarkt, Nostalgic Christmas market, is located not far from the Rotes Rathaus between the Staatsoper and Opernpalais on Unter den Linden. The atmosphere here is cosier as the 200 stalls nestle between the buildings.
At the nostalgic Christmas market around St. Hedwig's Cathedral, artisans and craftsmen present a great selection of high-quality Christmas gifts, decorations and culinary delights. Visitors will find anything from traditional tree decorations to lambskin slippers on the market, including nativity figurines, handcrafted toys, wood carvings and beeswax candles. Christmas music, traditional rides and the smell of festive delicacies help visitors get into the Christmas spirit.

A speciality of the Christmas market are the craftsmen on site: Lantern makers, chandlers, bakers and wood carvers demonstrate their crafts while the market-goers can watch them work and buy their products.

At the food stands, traditional Christmas foods such as hot roasted chestnuts, ginger bread, candied almonds, mulled wine, punch and some Tyrolean delicacies are available. For entertainment, a small number of historic fairground rides is set up.

Potsdamer Platz
10am – 10pm Daily

www.winterwelt-berlin.de

The market at Potsdamer Platz and in the Sony Centre and is a feast of lights, music and handicrafts. The Salzburger Schmankerl-Hütt'n offers you traditional Austrian foods in a ski hut that can host 230 guests. Visitors can watch the craftspeople at work and sample German and Austrian Christmas foods such as candied apples, roasted almonds and mulled wine. At the weekend, live music and an après-ski party atmosphere dominate the Christmas market at Potsdamer Platz.

Nearby on Alte Potsdamer Strasse is "Winter World" where you can sled down the largest mobile toboggan run or perhaps try the outdoor skating rink, or you can try your hand at Eisstockschiessen (like curling). The Winter World is open from early November until the end of December.

Breitscheidplatz
11am – 9pm Daily (10pm Friday and Saturday)

This market is centred around the Kaiser Wilhelm Memorial Church and the 100 stalls give you plenty of choice for souvenirs. Here you can buy hot roasted chestnuts or almonds and wash then down with the obligatory Glühwein. There are more than 10 variations of Glühwein as well as Eggnog and foods from all over Europe to keep you going as you wander around this market. Over 2 million visitors come to this market every year and see the 20-metre-high Christmas tree. There are also around 70 fairground rides to keep the younger family members entertained. From here you can continue your shopping along the Kurfürstendamm, either before or after the market.

Schloss Charlottenburg
2pm – 10pm Monday to Thursday
Midday – 10pm Friday to Sunday

If you want to venture ever so slightly further from the city centre, the Schloss Charlottenburg Christmas Market is lovely and the setting around the castle and gardens is particularly atmospheric. Along with a nice selection of things to buy at the 250 stalls, there are three restaurant tents, one selling local dishes from Brandenburg, one selling Austrian specialties and one selling mainly duck and goose-based dishes. You can take a horse and carriage ride around the park and gardens.

Berlin Sweets Market
Kreuzberg
First Sunday in December
Midday to 6pm

Located at the Markthalle IX in Kreuzberg, the Naschmarkt derives its name from the German verb naschen ("to nibble") and offers the opportunity to sample sweets from local vendors. The Naschmarkt is one-stop shop for the sweetest cakes, pies, tarts, brownies, scones, cupcakes, cookies, macaroons, marshmallows, chocolates, honeys and jams Germany's capital has to offer.

Scandinavian Market
3pm – 10pm Monday to Friday
1pm – 10pm Weekends

At the KulturBrauerei on Prenzlauer Berg you will find the Scandinavian market, which offers gifts from Norway, Denmark and Sweden, so if you fancy something a little bit different this could be the one for you.

Neukölln
There are different markets on the district of Neukölln taking place on the weekends in Advent

Alt Rixdorf
Second weekend in Advent
The nostalgic Christmas market around Richardplatz in the heart of Neukölln is open to visitors for one weekend only. At this time, Richardplatz, an old market square in the former Bohemian village Rixdorf, is decorated with paraffin lamps and other historic elements. In the glow of the historic oil lamps, over 200 vendors offer carefully curated Christmas decorations, foods and more. Among them are handmade toys, tree decorations and dipped candles. Honey, homemade jams, brushes, greeting cards are available at the stands and so are Bratwurst, candied apples, candy floss, mulled wine, hot chocolate and mead.

Other attractions at the Rixdorf Christmas market include pony riding, a visit of the Three Wise Men with their camels, a historic smithy and a display of historic carriages. Santa Claus, a historic police force and a witch do their best to entertain the little ones.

The Rixdorf Christmas market is a charitable event. Proceeds benefit neighbourhood initiatives in Neukölln.

Nordic Fairytale at Britz Palace
2nd and 3rd Weekends in December
The artists of the travelling theatre "Cocolorus Budenzauber" transform the site of the historic Christmas market into a fairy-tale landscape and perform a lovingly and heart-warming Christmas programme for young and old.

There are over 50 Christmas stalls and many activities to experience, such as rides with sledge dogs, pony rides, archery and crossbow shooting, a wooden water wheel, large impressive Viking boats for climbing and the "Dragon's Hammer", a large hand-operated music box.

Among the delicacies to eat are baked almonds, apple doughnuts and crepes. The drinks range from red and white mulled wine, medieval spiced wine, hot quince mead to the Scandinavian mulled punch Glögi. For the children there is traditionally hot elderberry punch.

Eco Market
Sophienstrasse
Saturday Midday to 8pm
Sunday 11am to 7pm

On the four weekends in Advent, environmental organisations, artists and designers with an ecological outlook sell their products at the Eco Christmas market at Sophienstrasse near Hackesche Höfe. As well as browsing through carefully selected Christmas gifts, visitors get to enjoy organic bratwurst, pies, waffles, vegan dishes and mulled wine. The products on offer include hip and trendy designer items and handicraft made in Berlin as well as all kinds of natural, organic and fair-trade items that make great Christmas gifts. Brass bands, stilt walkers and Santa Claus add to the festive atmosphere.

Spandau
www.partner-fuer-spandau.de
This market is outside the city centre in Spandau Old Town but is worth a mention as it is the largest market with 250 stalls during the week and 400 at weekends – so you won't be short of ideas for gifts. The Christmas market in Spandau is one of the most traditional and most beautiful in Berlin. Around the St. Nikolai church, a historic market with artisans and craftsmen is set up. Outside this market, fairground, musicians and entertainers help visitors get into the Christmas spirit. A stage programme including sing-alongs with Santa Claus, who also collects Christmas wishes, are aimed at the younger market-goers. Amongst the other attractions of this market are a manger scene with live animals, the St Nikolai Christmas Garden, the historic market at Reformationsplatz and entertainment such live rock music on Fridays at 6pm. Wednesday is family day.

Top Tip:
The weather in Berlin does get quite cold during winter, it is not unusual for temperatures to drop to well below freezing in December, so it is worth packing plenty of warm clothes. I suggest either one thick jacket or several layers is a good idea (inside restaurants etc. will be warm so you may want to take some layers off then) and I always like to have a nice pair of gloves and a warm hat too. You may also get snow, especially later in December and it does mean it may get a bit slippery underfoot, though pavements on larger roads tend to get swept and gritted quite regularly, so taking a warm pair of shoes or boots with good grips is a good idea.

What You Can Buy

There are many traditional specialties to buy in the markets. You will usually find that the stalls will specialize in one type of gift or product.

Wooden Gifts

The tradition of wooden gifts dates back many centuries and is as popular today as they were then. The gifts are still made in Oberammergau and the Erzgebirge as they were then.

Wooden smokers come in various designs. At this time of year, the theme is mainly for Christmas but if you visit Kathe Wohlfahrt and a shop in the Nikolai quarter they offer smokers for all seasons and occasions. You will find many different incense cones with different smells for you to put in your smoker such as pine or cinnamon. The smoke will then drift out of the mouth or hat or similar of the smoker. These give the room a lovely Christmas feeling. The incense is intended to remind the owner of the incense taken by the Three Wise Men to Bethlehem.

Wooden nutcrackers stand as soldiers and can vary in height, from about 6 inches to almost 2 feet high. Nuts are a popular festive snack in Germany and therefore the nutcracker is still a festive favourite.

There are various wooden toys on offer. You will find puzzles, trains, cars and animals as well as miniature wooden dolls house furniture.

Ceramics

Ceramic gifts include dishes, cups and plates for all year round as well as a festive selection. A very popular item is ceramic houses in which you can place a tea light candle to light it up as decoration on your fireplace or as a table centrepiece

Tree Ornaments

As you would expect there is a vast choice of Christmas tree ornaments and these can be made from a variety of materials. When you see the number of ornaments on some of the stalls it doesn't bear thinking about how long it takes them to set the stall up!

Straw is a common material for ornaments. You will find stars, angels and globes all made from straw. Straw was readily available centuries ago as a material to make decorations and can also be said to represent the stable.

Glass decorations come in all sizes and shapes. You will see round decorations, tear drop shapes and tree toppers. Some will be plain in colour and others will have winter scenes painted on them. Glass icicles in various colours are on sale. Look out for unusual metal hangers for the ornaments.

As you would expect you could also buy ornaments made from wood. These include snowmen, angels, houses, stars and countless more designs. The ornaments can either be plain wood or painted.

A very popular material for ornaments is pewter. You will find a large selection of themes and a year specific ornament, as well as a Berlin ornament. Everyone needs an angel for the top of the tree. Here you will find them made of wood, glass and straw as well as those with cloth dresses. The gold wings are to symbolize a guardian angel.

Other Handicrafts

In parts of Europe it is usual to see tables decorated with beautiful Christmas cloths. From small ones to fit under a table lamp to large cloths for the Christmas table. Usually lace is involved as well as delicate embroidery.

Candles are a big part of Christmas in most households. You will find many stalls selling candles and candleholders in all shapes, sizes and colours. There will also be small glass bowls with a winter or Christmas scene painted on them for you to place tea lights in

Lace and embroidered table linens are also very popular gifts, and these can be found in the market but also around the Nikolai quarter.

There will also be a great number of stalls selling food and drink souvenirs such as Lebkuchen (soft gingerbread), chocolates, cakes such as Stollen and perhaps some fruit brandies.

Apart from the markets the shops and department stores will have Christmas departments full of gifts and the food halls will offer chocolates, cakes such as Stollen and Lebkuchen and you will find bottles of Glühwein to take home.

Kathe Wohlfahrt
Ku'Damm 225
www.kaethe-wohlfahrt.de
Mon – Sat 10am to 7pm
Sunday 1pm to 5pm

This shop is part of the well-known company throughout Germany and Europe for its beautiful Christmas decorations that are available all year round. Whether you are looking for modern or traditional, wood, pewter or glass this shop has it all. You can find ornaments, traditional smokers, nativity scenes, Christmas village scenes and tableware. Keep walking down the Kurfürstendamm until you see the 2 giant nutcrackers and you are there.

Tastes of the Market

While wandering through the markets you may be enticed by the delicious smells of hot food and drink that is available. You will most likely find at least one selling Bratwurst, Pommes (chips or fries), often alongside the Berlin specialty the Bulette, a large flat pork meatball. Gulaschsuppe (goulash soup) is worth looking out for, as is Berliner Kartoffelsuppe (Berlin potato soup), both of which are usually not particularly expensive, but very filling and warming. If you prefer something more on the sweet side, you will usually find a stall selling Schmalzkuchen, which could be literally translated as 'lard cake' which sounds disgusting, but it is small squares of deep-fried dough, almost like little doughnuts. It is served in a cone of paper, covered with icing sugar. Crepes are also a popular sweet treat.

You will find many stalls selling Glühwein (warm mulled wine) and Feuerzangenbowle.

The Glühwein is spiced with cinnamon and other spices and is delicious. It is also possible to get a non-alcoholic version, Kinderpunsch, which is good for drivers or younger members of the family as it tastes almost the same but without the alcohol. Sometimes you may be offered your Glühwein "mit Schuss" which means would you like an extra shot of something added to it, usually rum or amaretto. The Feuerzangenbowle is a warm rum punch that has a sugar cone hanging above and slowly melts dripping the sugar into the punch. Other warm drinks such as hot chocolate is also available and may also be offered "mit Schuss'.

Top Tip:
You will pay a deposit (Pfand) of usually a couple of euros for your Glühwein cup. The cup then must be returned to the stall it was purchased from for a refund of the deposit (all stalls have different designs), alternatively it is perfectly acceptable for you to keep the cup as a souvenir without refund of the deposit. A cheap souvenir.

Christmas Food

Food is an essential and favourite part of everyone's festive season.

In the markets you smell the enticing spices of the gingerbread that is available. Popular gingerbread biscuits are Lebkuchen, originally from Nuremberg. You will see many packets of these biscuits some with icing upon them. The crisp outside reveals a soft, spicy gingerbread interior.

Gingerbread houses have long been associated as part of a German Christmas. You may not find any on the market to buy but you will certainly see kits in the shops for you to build them.

Gingerbread hearts are available all year in Germany. You will be able to buy them with a message already written on in coloured icing or perhaps have your own message put on. Stollen, a type of light fruit Christmas cake is available to buy. Dusted with icing sugar it can be plain or filled with marzipan.

Naturally there is a good selection of sweets and chocolates on sale. You can choose from jellies, small chocolates for children, Turkish delight and pralines. These do not normally come in packets but are loose for you to buy as much or little as you want. In the shops and stores you will see chocolate Santa's and reindeers in all sizes.

Other Events around the Christmas

Christmas Garden in Berlin
Botanical Gardens
Königin-Luise Platz
Mid-November to early January

Daily 4.30pm – 10pm

Inspired by "Christmas in Kew" in England, Christmas Garden Berlin invites visitors to a relaxing and enchanting stroll in Berlin's Botanical Garden. For almost eight weeks the two-kilometre tour features over a million light spots, colourful illuminations and Christmas-themed 3D figures all over the grounds. There are also warm and cosy fireplaces with local Christmas food treats. Those who would like to be more active can enjoy themselves on the ice rink. The Christmas Garden is a great family treat.

Christmas Concerts
Berlin Dom

In the atmospheric surroundings of the Dom, you can listen to a variety of concerts during the advent season. Check website for details.

Berlin Christmas Circus
Olympiastadion
Mid-December to early January

For 25 years this has been a treat for all then family. Great entertainment from clowns and jugglers as well as circus animals.

Eisstockschiessen
This traditional winter sport is popular all over Germany. Like curling, once the winter comes most towns and cities open their Eisstock lanes to customers.
Here are a couple of places you can give this a try in central Berlin:

Boulevard on Unter Den Linden
Café am Neuen See in Tiergarten
Potsdamer Platz

Ice Skating
Another family favourite in wintertime in Germany. In Berlin there is ice skating at Potsdamer Platz and at the rink at Charlottenburg.

New Year's Eve at Brandenburg Gate

On New Year's Eve, the city of Berlin invites guests and Berliners alike to celebrate the beginning of a new year with a huge open-air party. The celebrations with live bands, DJs and a spectacular firework display at midnight are free of charge and attract hundreds of thousands of people every year. The ensuing party continues until the early morning hours of New Year's Day.

The New Year's Eve celebrations take place on a two-kilometre long stretch of "Strasse des 17. Juni" between Brandenburg Gate and the Victory Column. The festival programme includes several live music performances, light and laser shows, and DJ sets. Along the festival area, food stands offer snacks from all over the world.

On New Year's Eve, gates open at 14:00. Between 14:00 and 18:30 that day, visitors can witness several live rehearsals for the evening. The official entertainment programme starts at 19:00. The fireworks are ignited at midnight, the party kicks off at 00:30 and continues until 03:00 in the morning of the New Year.

Please be aware there are strict security checks in place.

Shopping in Berlin

It is not just the culture and architecture that attract visitors to Berlin; many come here for a shopping trip too. Whether you are searching for souvenirs or a treat for yourself, whether you are following a shopping plan or just want to wander at will Berlin has a lot to offer from major shopping roads and centres to smaller streets and districts. In Mitte, most shoppers favour the areas around Friedrichstrasse, Potsdamer Platz and Alexanderplatz whilst further west a visit to the most famous street Kurfürstendamm with the Europa-Center and KaDeWe close by are a must.

You could find yourself tempted by the many beautiful products available from fashion, jewellery and accessories, art, books, crafts and foods, gifts to suit every pocket. For those wanting luxury items then Friedrichstrasse and Unter den Linden are the areas for you with boutiques and international designers such as Yves Saint Laurent. For the collectors among you, many antique shops can be found in Schöneberg (Keithstrasse and Fuggerstrasse and Charlottenburg Savignyplatz, Suarezstrasse and Damaschstrasse).

There are many arts, antique and flea markets around the city, the largest is in the Strasse des 17 Juni on Saturday and Sunday. There is an antique and flea market, with over 100 stalls, in the SBahn bridges at Friedrichstrasse station. Also, worth a visit are the many grocery and produce markets held throughout the city, which often include crafts, and the most well-known of these are found at Winterfeldtplatz in Schöneberg and the Kollwitzmarkt on Thursday and Saturday.

There are many souvenir shops around Berlin selling the usual variety of gifts; postcards, t-shirts, books etc. and these will usually feature scenes from Berlin or the word BERLIN itself. Other gifts may feature the city symbol of a brown bear or the traffic crossing man known locally as "Ampelmann" and is now a cult hero. You will also find alleged pieces of the Berlin Wall; however, I am not convinced these are genuine after all this time

Most stores are open from 10am to 8pm but not on Sundays when all stores are closed. Here are some of the main shopping areas and stores.

Kurfürstendamm
Ranked in the German Tourist Board "Top 100 Sights in Germany"

The Kurfürstendamm, or Ku'damm to the locals is probably Berlin's best-known shopping street. It is a wide boulevard stretching for 3.5 kilometres and has a tree lined central promenade. Along the street you will find department stores, luxury boutiques and small independent stores. Mix these with cafes and restaurants and you have a wonderful day out.

Friedrichstrasse

For an exclusive shopping experience in Mitte try the Friedrichrichstadtpassagen and its 'Quartiers'. Quartier 206 for international designer wear in an art deco atmosphere or the French emporium Galeries Lafayette, in Quartier 207. This spectacular building is known for its stunning luminous glass cone in the entrance. More stores and a large food hall with abundant international specialties in Quartier 205 provide an ideal lunch-break stopover. The three buildings are located between the subway stations "Stadt Mitte" and "Französische Strasse".

Alexanderplatz
Ranked a German National Tourist Board "Top 100 Sights in Germany"

The Alexanderplatz is probably one of the best-known squares in Berlin and was great for shopping from the beginning. The construction of the Zentrale Markthalle (1886) and the Tietz department store (1904–1911) made the square an important shopping centre. In the 1960's the former Centrum-Warenhaus and the Alex Passages were built, and the area became a pedestrian zone. After reunification, the Centrum Warenhaus was converted into the modern Galeria Kaufhof. In 2007 the Alexa shopping centre was opened and two years later Die Mitte shopping centre also opened, so nowadays, there is nothing you can't buy at the "Alex".

Hackescher Markt

The Hackescher Markt and Hackesche Höfe (courtyards) are a great place to head for a lively mix of shops, bars and cafés. Set away from mainstream boulevards this is the place to soak in Berlin's local, trendy atmosphere. The district, known as Scheunenviertel, along Schönhauser Strasse is a magnet for those looking for smaller shops, indie fashion labels or outrageous shoes. It is a great corner of former East Berlin bustling with energy, creativity and innovative spirit.

Schlossstrasse
Schlosstrasse 1
www.schlossstrasse-hat-es.de

Schlossstrasse in Steglitz is the real deal in shopping streets in Berlin with over 800 shops in the area. There is an exciting assortment of small shopping centres, department stores and individual stores along the 1.5 kilometres. When your feet are tired you can take a break in one of the many cafes and restaurants that are interspersed among the shops.

Europa-Center
Tauentzienstrasse
www.europa-center-berlin.com

The Europa-Center is located on the site of the former Romanische café, where many literary greats used to meet before the Second World War, and adjacent the Kaiser Wilhelm Church. The centre was opened in 1965 and today this glass and aluminium structure is a listed building. The centre offers shoppers over 70 shops, restaurants and cafes all under one roof. However, it is not just the shops that attract the tens of thousands of visitors each day there are also many sights for you to see too including the World Fountain, the Water Clock, sections of the Berlin wall and the Lotus Clock. On the roof of the centre, the Mercedes Star, the largest of its kind in the World, acts as a guide to bring you here and has not stopped rotating since its inception in 1965.

Potsdamer Platz Arkaden
Potsdamer Platz

The Potsdamer Platz Arkaden was an integral part of the planning of the Potsdamer Platz itself. There are numerous different events that make this arcade stand out from the crowd, alongside the shops is a variety of ways including restaurants for the visitors to enjoy themselves. The arcade is a successful blend of architecture, shopping, arts, events and gastronomy.

Schönhauser Allee Arkaden
Schönhauser Allee 79
www.schoenhauser-allee-arcaden.de

This shopping centre is in the heart of Prenzlauer Berg, located on the Schönhauser Allee itself. It is not only popular with visitors it is much favoured by locals and the streets around the centre offer a chance for some retail therapy too. There are over 100 shops and stores over 3 floors for you to wander around and find that special gift.

Der Clou
Kurt-Schumacher-Damm 1-15
www.derclouberlin.de

Der Clou has an attractive variety of stores for you to browse around, over 50 in fact, and offers a wide assortment of products for you to buy. There are also many restaurants and cafes for you to take a well-earned break from your shopping. Der Clou is well known for hosting events throughout the year and these include child-focused events, Easter and Christmas Markets.

Hallen am Borgisturm
Am Borgisturm 2
www.hallenamborgisturm.de

This shopping centre was opened in 2000 on the site where August Borsig once built his famous steam locomotive. There are over 120 shops from major chains to smaller independent stores. For relaxation you can enjoy the many cafes and restaurants or perhaps visit the bowling alley or cinema.

Forum Köpenick
Bahnhofstrasse 33-38
www.forum-koepenick.de

In Berlin's woodland district of Köpenick is one of the city's larger and more appealing shopping centres. Built in 1997, there are over 140 shops for you to browse through and over 20 cafes and restaurants selling everything from ice cream to pizza and pasta. There is always something new happening with changing decorations and events.

KaDeWe
Wittenbergplatz
www.kadewe.de
Ranked in the German Tourist Board "Top 100 Sights in Germany"

What began as an adventurous idea by the Berlin merchant Adolf Jandorf in 1905 surpassed all expectations when KaDeWe was opened in March 1907. As the leading department store in the country, it presented customers with an assortment of desirable goods from around the world and today the store is the largest department store on mainland Europe. Every day at KaDeWe and occasionally on Sundays too, shortly before 10 am, the original iron gate dating from 1907 is opened so that customers can embark on an exciting shopping adventure over the stores 6 floors and each day up to 180,000 customers from around the world are welcomed in to the store. In its world-famous food hall on the sixth floor there are thousands of foodie treats for you to choose from and the smells that drift through the sir tempt you from one counter to the next.

Karstadt
Kurfürstendamm 231
www.karstadt.de

The Karstadt department store near the Memorial Church offers modern shopping in the best department store tradition. The store offers a fantastic selection and variety of goods offering everything from the top trends in fashion to the latest lifestyle items, from luxury furniture to fresh culinary delicacies. With top offers on quality brands and a special tip for connoisseurs: the café-restaurant on the 6th floor offers a wonderful view over the rooftops of Berlin

Galeria Kaufhof
Alexanderplatz
www.galeria-kaufhof.de

The Galeria Kaufhof, located centrally in the eastern city centre, offers a distinguished range of goods aimed at an international clientele, and is the flagship of the Galeria Kaufhof chain. The entrepreneur Herman Tietz was the first to build a store on the site, which was destroyed during the Second World War. The current building was constructed between 1967 to house the HO-Centrum department store, the largest in East Berlin. After reunification, the building was refurbished beginning in 2004 and an atrium was added, roofed by a large glass dome. The store opened in 2006 and boasts a total of 20 escalators with a length of up to 24 metres, some of the largest cantilevered escalators in any department store in the world.
Shoppers can explore numerous designer shops arranged over 35,000 square metres. The focus is not only on trendy fashion and life style goods, but also features a large delicatessen department.

Galeries Lafayette
Friedrichstrasse 76
www.galerieslafayette.de

In 1996 Galeries Lafayette made the leap from Paris to the Spree. The first German branch was built on the corner of Friedrichstrasse and Französische Strasse, just a few minutes from Unter den Linden. The Parisian store had its sights set to be on Berlin's retail map for some time and after endless pulling down of old buildings, new building works and restoration, on the new Friedrichstrasse was also a new glossy building. Jean Nouvel's glass masterpiece and its main tenants, Galeries Lafayette, was the first noticeable symbol for the Friedrichstadt Passages and the other shops to follow.

Käthe Wohlfahrt
Kurfürstendamm 225/226
www.kaethe-wohlfahrt.com

Here it is Christmas all year round! In this delightful shop you can be captured by the festive season in the "Christmas Wonderland" whatever the time of year. Thousands of traditional German Christmas decorations, wooden nutcrackers, incense smokers and ornaments made from wood, glass and most famously pewter. However, as well as Christmas decorations you will find a selection of seasonal gifts too. Kathe Wohlfahrt is probably Germany's best-known Christmas tradition and you should make it part of your too.

Leysieffer
Friedrichstrasse 68
Kurfürstendamm 218
Schlossstrasse 26
6th floor KaDeWe

For more than 100 years, hand-made chocolate truffles, Baumkuchen and chocolate bars with exotic, unusual and very special flavours such as chilli or sea salt have been sent by Leysieffer all over the world. Quality comes first for the heavenly chocolate truffles, chocolate bars, Baumkuchen, gingerbread cookies and all the other mouth -watering sweets. High quality, natural ingredients, skillfully handmade products and production on demand stand for unbelievable indulgence. There are also cafes in the stores in KaDeWe and Friedrichstrasse.

Steiff
38/39 Kurfürstendamm
www.steiff.de

A branch of this world-famous teddy bear brand ensures you can have that extra special little gift to take home with you. The bears with their famous "Knopf im Ohr' or "Button in ear" are recognized around the world and have proven to be collector's items as well as much loved toys. Here there is a great selection to choose from as well as other items such as clothing that you may not see in department stores.

Food and Drink

Food in Berlin is home cooked, hearty and delicious. There is a huge selection of international restaurants available which reflects the multi-cultural citizens of the city, whether it is Turkish, Chinese or Indian you fancy, you will not be short of choice of restaurant.

However, it is on German food I will focus on as my belief is wherever you are in the world you should eat like a local. In Berlin there is food to fit every pocket, from fast food to top class restaurants. Local specialties include Eisbein, which is smoked pork knuckle and usually served with Sauerkraut (white cabbage), Buletten – a type of large pork meatball / burger and Currywurst – a sausage served with a curry powder on top. Potatoes also feature high on menus either as pancakes served with a variety of accompaniments, fried (Bratkartoffeln) or perhaps in the local recipe version of soup. You will find quite a lot of fish on the menu and favourites are herring, either as a main course or as a snack like Roll mops.

Those with a sweet tooth are not forgotten, Berliner are a sweet doughnut and a must have at Fasching and New Year's Eve or perhaps you prefer Spritzkuchen which are cream filled puffs like a choux bun.

For Berliners a highlight of the week is Sunday Brunch, often served until mid-afternoon. You will find many restaurants offer, "as much as you can eat" buffet for the Brunch for a set price. During the week many restaurants offer daily specials, especially at lunchtime, which are good value for money.

When you enter a restaurant, it is not always usual for the waiter to come and seat you, it is more often you find your own table. Do not be surprised that if the restaurant is busy that you find other people it down at the table with you, this is common all over Germany.

Fast food stands (Imbiss) are all over the city, particularly at stations and often provide a good quality snack such as Pommes (fries or chips), sandwiches or Currywurst.

Beer is favourite in Berlin, just as elsewhere in Germany, and the common local brew is Berliner Weisse. This is not as strong beer, only around 3% and is often served "mit Schuss". On this occasion you will be offered Rote Berliner (red with a shot of raspberry), Gelb (yellow with a shot of lemon) or Grüne (green with a shot of Woodruff). Another local beer is the Berliner Kindl, which has been brewed here since 1870.

There are various types of beer available in Berlin; Helles, Dunkeles and Weizen.

A **Helles** is the most popular beer and is what you will be given if you just ask for a beer. It is a pale golden lager type beer, cool and refreshing with a large foamy head. Often served in one-litre glass steins (a Mass) it contains fewer calories than the equivalent measure of milk or fruit juice. The strength is usually 4.5/5%, however special brews are stronger. When mixed with lemonade it is known as a radler (shandy).

Dunkeles (Dark Beer) has a higher concentration of malt, which gives it its darker colour. This can also be served in one-litre steins and has strength of about 4/4.5%

Bock Beer is mainly brewed for celebratory seasons such as Starkbierzeit (Strong Beer Season) or Maibock in May. The bock beers usually end with "ator" such as Salvator and can be 6-7% strength.

Weiss or Weizen (Wheat Beer) is the most popular non-lager type beer. It is poured from bottles into tall thin glasses and can be very refreshing on warm days. It is a cloudy beer of up to 6% strength. When mixed with lemonade it is known as russ'n.

Schnapps is a distilled liqueur of 32% or above. In the north of Germany, it is usually made from grain such as corn but in the south fruits such as apples, pears, plums and cherries are used. Obstler or Obstwasser is often a combination of apples and pears. Jägermeister, which is a combination of grain and herbs, is found on most menus too.

There are many small microbreweries in Berlin and many of these have Stübe (rooms or bars) where you can have a beer and some food. Here is a selection.

Brauhaus Lemke
Hackescher Markt
www.brauhaus-lemke.com
Midday to Midnight Daily

First opened in the arches under the viaduct in 1999 and just 2 minutes' walk from Alexanderplatz, this brewery has over 40 different beers on offer including seasonal and monthly specials. There is a large menu with pork and beef dishes, salads, vegetarian and seafood all available for you to try. There is a lunchtime special of an "all you can eat" buffet on weekdays at midday.

Brauhaus Lemke am Schloss
Luisenplatz / Dirckenstrasse

www.brauhaus-lemke.de
Midday to Midnight Daily

The sister restaurant of the Brauhaus in Hackescher Markt, this is Berlin's oldest brewery tavern and full of rustic charm. The restaurant opened in its current form opposite Charlottenburg in 1987. Delicious home cooked food accompanies the refreshing beer and the restaurant is conveniently located in Mitte.

Brauhaus Lemke am Alex
Karl-Liebnecht Strasse 13
Midday to Midnight Daily

The latest addition to this brewing family of restaurants, located in Alexanderplatz close to the TV tower

Brauhaus Südstern
Hasenheide 69
www.brauhaus-suedstern.de

This is a local brewery and since 2006 the only brewery in Kreuzberg; you can book a brewery tour with the Master Brewer, which includes beer tasting. The interior is rustic brickwork and can seat up to 180 guests. There are occasionally live music events and a beer garden outside in Hasenheide Park for the summer months. The menu includes a good value Sunday brunch between 10am and 2pm with hot and cold food choices for you. The beer is a traditional unfiltered (cloudy) beer.

Georgbrau
Spreeufer 4
www.georgbraeu.de

This brewery is in the Nikolai quarter and can seat 280 people inside and 400 in the beer garden that overlooks the River Spree. First opened in 1992 it is easy to identify by the green and gold garden umbrellas outside. The menu offers traditional Berlin dishes as well as fish and salads. The house specialty is "Brauhaus Hit" which is Eisbein, peas, sauerkraut and potatoes all accompanied by a Georg Pils and schnapps.

Brauhaus in Rixdorf
Glasower Strasse 27

This brewery is in an original villa in Neukölln. There are several beers available as well as seasonal beers. Food is good and hearty, and Tuesday is Schnitzel day.

Eschenbräu
Triftstrasse 67
www.eschenbraeu.de

Here you can drink a different beer for every season; spring means its Maibock time, summer is Red wedding, autumn is Panke Gold and in winter there is a strong beer Old Swede. There is room for 100 guests inside and 200 in the beer garden in summer. There is a variety of fruit schnapps available for you to try or buy. A specialty of the house is Flammkuchen, a wafer-thin pizza type base topped with onions and bacon.

Hops and Barley
Wühlischstrasse 38
www.hopsandbarley-berlin.de

There are several beers available here including monthly specials as well as the fruity house cider, all of which are served unfiltered and therefore have a cloudy appearance. Specialty drinks of the house include Schlangenbiss, which is half beer, half cider with a shot of fruit syrup, or perhaps a Diesel, which is a mix of beer and cola. An unusual item on the food menu is bread and dripping with bockwurst.

Brauhaus in Spandau
Neuendorfer Strasse 1
www.brauhaus-spandau.de

Located in a traditional red brick building this brewery has a new beer specialty every month. You can have breakfast here until 2pm and the menu includes many Berlin dishes. There is also a hotel here for you to stay.

Favourite Restaurants and Beer Gardens

Restaurants will usually have menus in English, ask for "an Englischer Karte, bitte" and there are often smaller portions for children.

Hofbräuhaus Berlin
Karl-Liebnecht-Strasse 30
www.berlin-hofbraeu.de

The Hofbräu in Berlin opened its doors in November 2011 and has been synonymous with Bavarian spirit in the capital ever since. Enjoy a nice cool original Hofbräu beer served in "Mass Krug" and a comprehensive range of Bavarian specialties and the staff, dressed in dirndl and lederhosen also ensures you forget that you are in Berlin and not the original in Munich. The traditional entertainment is provided by several bands of the original Hofbräuhaus Show who play in every Hofbräuhaus around the world. A must and not just for fans of Bavaria.

Experience the live band at the following times:
Afternoons: Mon - Sat 12:00 - 15:00 and Sun 10:00 - 15:00
Evenings: Sun - Thurs 18:00 - 23:00 and Fri - Sat 19:00 - 24:00

Metzer Eck
Metzer Strasse 33
www.metzer-eck.de

This is the oldest tavern in Prenzlauer Berg and has been here since 1913. It is full of atmosphere and cosy. The menu is small but still offers local favourites such as sausages and Buletten at very reasonable prices. Closed on Sundays.

November
Husemannstrasse 15
www.cafe-november.de

Another restaurant in Prenzlauer Berg and has been a favourite with the locals for 20 years for its traditional local fare. They offer a fantastic breakfast menu from 9am to around 4pm and could be a good way to start your day.

Schwarzwaldstueben
Tucholskystrasse 48

You will find this restaurant in many guides and listings as it offers a great atmosphere accompanied by great food, traditional menu favourites such as Schnitzel, sausages, beef and steaks.

Schildkroete
Kurfürstendamm 212
www.restaurant-schildkroete.de

This restaurant has been here since 1936 and its walls are covered with wood panelling and sets of antlers hang from the walls. The menu is extensive with soups, fish, game, steaks, seasonal and daily specials and a children's menu. There is a lunch time special from midday to 4pm on weekdays for around 7 euros. The restaurant considers the duck, goose, Eisbein and Haxe to be house specialties.

Radke Gasthaus Alt Berlin
Marburger Strasse 16
www.alt-berlin.de

This traditional Old Berlin restaurant offers local and regional food in a warm and friendly atmosphere. Located conveniently near the UBahn station Zoo, the restaurant can sit 100 inside and on warmer days 30 outside. There are many house specialties including the pork knuckle; the stuffed cabbage roll with 500g of meat inside; veal liver and pork loin.

Alt Berliner Biersalon
Kurfürstendamm 225
www.alt-berliner-biersalon.de

Centrally located on the Ku'damm, there has been a restaurant on this site for around 100 years. The restaurant is popular with locals and visitors alike and the menu offers both local specialties as well as continental favourites such as nachos and pasta dishes, all at reasonable prices. Today the biersalon is open 24 hours a day and has screens to show live sports events. Also, for your entertainment is Karaoke at weekends.

Alt- Berliner Wirtshaus (Henne)
Leuschnerdamm 25
www.henne-berlin.de

This restaurant has been here for many, many years and is famous for inviting President Kennedy for a drink when he visited the city in 1963, and a signed picture of the President hangs behind the bar. The house specialty is chicken, often served with salad and potato salad and the salty crispy skin will give you the thirst and excuse (if you need one) for another beer.

Augustiner am Gendarmenmarkt
Charlottenstrasse 55 (corner Jagerstrasse)
www.augustiner-braeu-berlin.de
10am – 1am

Augustiner is the most popular brewery in Munich and this restaurant stays true to tradition. Wooden floors and tables, daily specials and the most fantastic beer. The food is hearty and delicious, from soups and snacks to full meals and desserts. There is a weekly specials menu for lunchtimes – but that does not mean the portions are small!

Lowenbrau at the Gendarmenmarkt
Leipzigerstrasse 65
www.loewenbraeuberlin.de
Mon – Sunday 11.30am – 1.30am

Newly refurbished, here you can sample not only the Lowenbrau beer but also that of Spaten and Franziskaner. There is a beer garden outside for the summer months and large screens inside for football and other sporting events. There is food to suit every appetite, from snacks and cold platters, soups or hearty main courses.

Maximilians
Friedrichstrasse 185 – 190
www.maximiliansrestaurant.de

Located not far from Potsdamer Platz this restaurant serves a mixture of Berlin and Bavarian food such as Haxe, roast pork and the obligatory sausages. You can have your beer served in a one-litre stein, a "Mass" if you prefer. There is a daily special lunchtime menu from 11.30am to 3pm and you can have the set main course with either a soup or dessert for less than 7 euros.

Bavarium
Tauentzienstrasse 9 – 12
www.bavarium-berlin.de

This traditional Bavarian restaurant is in the basement of the Europa Centre. The interior is full of charm with wooden tables, benches and chairs. The menu features Bavarian specialties such as Haxe, Schnitzel, Weisswurst and Obazda and the Munich beer Lowenbrau.

Xaneter Eck
Xaneter Strasse 1
www.das-xaneter-eck.de

Berliners and visitors alike have many reasons to visit this renowned restaurant and beer house. Daily from 9 am until 1 am typical Berlin cooking and excellent beers from several world-famous breweries are on draught. There is a good breakfast selection available in the mornings; excellent brunch on Sunday and good home cooked food throughout the remainder of the day. For many customers the Xaneter Eck reflects the cosmopolitan atmosphere of the city.

Kartoffelkeller
Albrechtstrasse 14b
www.kartoffelkeller.com

The Kartoffelkeller is centrally located in the government district, in historic Berlin cellars, and offers over 100 dishes inspired by the potato in truly cosy surroundings. The menu includes potato pancakes with a choice of accompaniments, various potato casseroles and potatoes fried, roasted or baked – there are even potatoes served as dessert. The quality and diversity of these unique dishes have enjoyed an excellent reputation since 1995.

Die Berliner Republik
Schiffbauerdamm 8
www.die-berliner-republik.de

Die Berliner Republik is a cosy bar located on the River Spree just minutes from the Reichstag and the Brandenburg Gate. The interior can sit up to 180 guests and there is an outdoor river side terrace. The food is typically Berlin style and they pride themselves on the home cooking "just like Grandma used to make".

However here is the novelty factor for this restaurant.
Every day at 5pm the regular beer prices are forgotten, and new prices are regulated by supply and demand, as on the real stock market.

The rules are easy to understand: your order is placed on the market computer, which permanently updates the price for each individual beer according to demand. This means that you can pay any price from EUR 1.60 upwards and there is no limit! The beers that are not in great demand are more reasonably priced and therefore find favour with the guests.

You can observe how the price of your favourite beer is developing on monitors all over the Berlin Republic, so that you know what you must pay when ordering. A good opportunity for speculators!! You pay the price which is shown on the monitor when you order. You then receive a coupon showing the price and the time zone when you placed your order. This is the price you pay when the waiter brings your beer, even if the price has risen in the meantime, partly of course due to the increase in demand your order has caused.

The market crash – good news for speculators!

Now and again, depending on the activities of the beer trade, the market crashes and the prices fall rapidly. So, make sure to watch the development of the courses on the monitor and place a quick order.

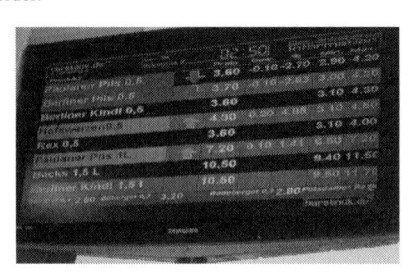

Markthalle
Puecklerstrasse 34
www.weltrestaurant-markthalle.de

This restaurant is within a former market hall and is therefore long and has high ceilings. The kitchen takes pride in the food it offers with a focus on German and Austrian specialties. The menu changes weekly but ever present are roast pork (Schweinebraten), Spaetzle (cheesy noodles) and apple strudel. This is also a good place for breakfast.

Zillemarkt
Bleibtreustrasse 48
www.zillemarkt.de

Since the turn of the century this restaurant in Charlottenburg, has been well known for its welcome and quality; nostalgic and modern are successfully combined here. Zille's heritage is ever-present in our traditional restaurant, the original glass facade which has been preserved, the cobbled surface of the floor and the old pharmacist sideboard that has now been altered to make the bar, represent more than 100 years of the restaurant's history. You can relax in this authentic nostalgic atmosphere and enjoy the delicious meals on offer from breakfast and throughout the day. There is a good selection of crepes for dessert. Alternatively, if you just fancy a mid-morning or mid-afternoon coffee, the coffee house serves delicious home-made cakes.

Sophieneck
Grosse Hamburgerstrasse 37
www.sophieneck-berlin.de

This traditional restaurant was originally opened as a bakery in 1924 by the Balzer family and passed through the family until in 1986 Traudel Balzer opened the premises as a restaurant, although the bakery remains. In 1994 the restaurant was sold to new owners. This restaurant is highly regarded by locals, which is always a good sign, and offers diners a good selection of regional and German favourites.

Zillestube
Spreeufer 3
www.zillestube-nikolaiviertel.de

Here is a true Berlin restaurant located right in the middle of Nikolaiviertel, the historic heart of the city and just a few steps away from Berlin's oldest structure, Nikolai Kirche or Church of St. Nicholas. Enjoy great food and discover some typical German dishes from the old Berlin in a relaxing historic atmosphere or perhaps some lovely fresh waffles for those with a sweet tooth.

Zur Letzen Instanz
Waisenstrasse 14-16
www.zurletzeninstanz.de

This is the oldest restaurant in Berlin and has been here in the Nikolaiviertel since 1600. The medieval building has been completely restored, but the annexes and the original interior have remained historically preserved. As you step on the old brick floor, you are taken back into the "good old days", and its local drawings, paintings and photographs tell even more stories of former days. The oldest and probably most popular piece of furniture, however, is the 200-year-old tiled stove, which folklore says on which Napoleon made himself comfortable and enjoyed culinary specialities. The menu contains all the usual favourites and is worth a visit.

Paulaners im Spreebogen
Alt-Moabit 98
www.paulaners-berlin.de

The famous Munich brewery Paulaner serves cool refreshing beer in this charming restaurant. The interior is wood panelled, rustic and friendly. The menu contains local specialties as well as Bavarian specialties such as Obazda and Weisswurst. The restaurant has seasonal events such as a special menu for Mother's Day, Asparagus Season and Oktoberfest when you can have the special Oktoberfest beer and listen to live music.

Restaurant Knese
Knesebeckstrasse 63

Just a short distance from the Kurfürstendamm this is a traditional local restaurant with a large sun terrace for the summer months. Specialties on the menu include Eisbein with Sauerkraut, Kartoffelsuppe and Wiener schnitzel.

Treffpunkt Berlin
Mittelstrasse 55

This small "Kneipe" is just a short distance from Friedrichstrasse and Unter den Linden. The restaurant describes itself as a place with a heart in the heart of the city. The menu represents traditional Berlin cooking in a friendly atmosphere.

Café am Neuen See
Liechtensteinallee 2

This is a beer garden in Tiergarten and located directly overlooking the water, a lovely location for a warm day and watching the boats. You can hire rowing boats here. The menu is not traditionally local, but you can enjoy a refreshing beer and a pizza.

Golgatha
Dudenstrasse 40
www.golgatha-berlin.de

For more than 30 years, Golgatha has been the place to be in Berlin-Kreuzberg and can offer the visitor a great variety. It is perhaps the place to be if you want to have an early coffee amidst the twittering birds of Viktoriapark, if you want to pick up some cake or ice cream for the playground, if you want to catch the day's last sunbeams on the sun terrace whilst sampling the beers, cocktails and delicious homemade food, or finally if you just want to dance until dawn to the a DJ.

Luise
Königin-Luise-Strasse 40
www.luise-dahlem.de

This restaurant was refurbished in 2001 and is open every day from breakfast until the early hours. The menu includes traditional dishes as well as an extensive pizza menu; Thursdays are "Student Days" with cheap offers for the local students. On Sundays and holidays there is a Sunday brunch which offers good value for money. There is a lovely beer garden in the summer.

Friedrichs 106
Friedrichstrasse 106
www.friedrichs106.de

This is a traditional coffee house in the heart of Berlin overlooking the River Spree. Open from 7am weekdays and 8am weekends their breakfast is a good way to start the day. However, the café should not be missed during the day for the fantastic range of homemade cakes and pastries all washed down with a delicious hot coffee.

Café Einstein
Kurfürstenstrasse 56

The traditional appearance of Café Einstein feels just like a fashionable Viennese coffeehouse, here first-class coffee is served on a tray in a friendly manner as you sit at a marble table amidst the pleasant smells of the cafe. In addition to its extensive breakfast offering, Café Einstein also has Austrian specialties such as apple strudel and Wiener schnitzel. The cakes are homemade and delicious, and the choice is endless.

Planes, Trains and Automobiles

Getting to Berlin

By Plane

Berlin has 2 airports, Tegel and Schönefeld and both airports are served by international airlines from around the world, either with direct or connecting flights. There are easy transfers into the city, which take around 30 minutes maximum from Schönefeld which is the furthest from the city.
www.berlin-airport.de

By Train

The Hauptbahnhof (Central Station) is in the centre of the city and is bright and modern. You can take a train to Berlin from almost anywhere, as it is Europe's largest interchange hub, therefore well connected to other cities around Europe. Tickets can be purchased online beforehand from Deutsche Bahn and the website is available in English.
www.bahn.de

By Coach

Many visitors come to Berlin by coach, from backpackers and travellers to school children and senior citizens; coach travel is often a cheap way to travel and see the country as you pass. National and international coach companies arrive and depart from the central coach station in Charlottenburg.

By Car

Berlin is well linked to the German Autobahn network and travel by car is relatively stress free. You will need an emissions sticker for your car for the city and these can be purchased online beforehand. These stickers do not just cover Berlin but every city in Germany, and most require you have them displayed on your vehicle. The cost is quite low, less than 10 euros.
www.berlin.de

Getting Around Berlin

Public transport in Berlin, like other German cities, is very good and excellent value for money. Whatever your destination in Berlin, you will find it easy and convenient to reach by public transport. You can travel by bus, UBahn and SBahn and tickets can be purchased that cover all three networks. The standard fare is for adults, children 6 – 15 years travel at reduced rates and the under 6's travel free of charge.

Most people will be visiting for a few days and a good value option is a City Tour Card that can be purchased either for 48-hour, 72 hour or 5-day duration and this gives you unlimited travel during this period. You can also buy single ticket for one journey, an all-day ticket or perhaps if there are a few of you a Small group Ticket which covers up to 5 adults.

The BVG covers the buses and the UBahn (www.bvg.de) and the SBahn covers the SBahn (www.s-bahn-berlin.de) these websites will give you more details on current prices and tickets.

Top Tip:
You must validate your ticket before you start your journey at the machines in the stations or stops, tickets can also be purchased and validated on board trams.

Sleep

Berlin has beds to suit every budget. There are over 350 hotels, hostels and guesthouses in the city as well as self-catering options too. Most people tend to choose to stay either around the Alexander Platz area or the area around the Kurfürstendamm either has a lot to offer – the choice is yours.

Useful Information

Tourist Information

The tourist information office can provide maps; help with last minute accommodation and book event tickets.

Hauptbahnhof
Daily 8am to 10pm

Brandenburg Gate
Daily 10am to 6pm

Neues Kranzler Eck (near zoo)
Monday - Saturday 10am to 8pm
Sunday 10am to 6pm (longer in summer)

Public Holidays in Berlin

On these days you will find most restaurants will be open, but all the shops and some attractions may be closed.

New Year's Day   (1st January)
Epiphany   (6th January)
Good Friday / Karfreitag
Easter Monday
May Day   (1st May)
Ascension
Whit Monday
Day of German Unity   (3rd October)
Christmas Day and Boxing Day

Emergency Numbers

Police   110
Fire   112
Medical   310031

British Embassy

Wilhelmstrasse 70
Tel: 030204570
consular@british-embassy.de
Weekdays 9am to Midday; 2pm to 4pm
Closed Wednesdays

US Embassy

Clayallee 170
03083050
No walk-in service

About the Author

Yvonne Salisbury was born in Newcastle upon Tyne, England, is married to Stephen and has two daughters. Yvonne has been visiting Germany for over 30 years, but it is to Berlin and Bavaria that her heart belongs. She has been visiting these beautiful areas with friends and family, several times a year for more than 15 years.

"My guides differ from others," says Yvonne "I have been and actually experienced what I write about, I started as a visitor myself and therefore believe I understand what the visitor needs to know".

In recent years Yvonne has created her own websites for these areas and written several guides as well as freelance articles for The Daily Telegraph and The Munich Times. She was voted Simonseeks "Writer of the Month" for November 2009 and is a travel expert for Guide Gecko on Munich and the Oktoberfest.

"I have visited the Oktoberfest for 15 years. It's so big, it's impossible to see it all in a single visit", says Yvonne Salisbury. "My Oktoberfest guide is ideal for first timers and lederhosen-veterans alike. Visit my site before you go, not to miss the best!"

Websites by Yvonne Salisbury, including details of how to buy guides, latest information on events and what is happening in and around each area:

www.insidersguide-online.com

Also by Yvonne Salisbury on Kindle

Beer, Bratwurst & Breze

You're not here for a long time, just a good time and Insiders' Guides show you how. All the detailed information you need is here about restaurants, shopping, and sightseeing. This is a must have volume for anyone really wanting to make the most of their Munich holiday.

Originally 3 guide books written by herself about Munich, Oktoberfest, Beer Gardens and their culture and the Christmas Markets, Yvonne has combined them all into this one handy book "Beer, Bratwurst and Breze". It includes details of many attractions for you to see, daytrips, walking tours, details of festivals throughout the year including Oktoberfest and the Christmas Markets, over 50 recommended restaurants and beer gardens and places to eat, many insider "top tips" and more than 100 photographs. The author visits Munich several times a year for over 25 years so she knows this subject well. All information has been gathered personally, not found on Wikipedia and such like, that's what makes our Insiders' Guides unique.

Written by Munich expert Yvonne Salisbury, it provides reviews, photographs, and advice for all the family, plus tips on what else to see and do in Munich and its surroundings.

Mozart, Maria & Mountains.

Originally 2 books written by herself, Yvonne has combined them under one title "Mozart, Maria and Mountains" to make this complete guide to the Bavarian Alps area around Salzburg and Berchtesgaden.

Salzburg is a compact city, despite being the fourth largest city in Austria. Situated at the edge of the Alps, most of Salzburg's main attractions are conveniently located near the old town. It is the old town that has the most charm with narrow streets that lead to cobbled squares. With castles, churches, markets and a variety of shops there is plenty to see and do in Salzburg. It is a beautiful city, famous for Mozart and The Sound of Music and declared a World Heritage Site by UNESCO in 1997. Since much of the old town is a pedestrian zone and relatively small, it is ideal for walking and window shopping – it only takes about 20 minutes to walk from one end to the other.

Nestling in the South East of the German Alps in the Berchtesgadener Land National Park, the Berchtesgaden is popular with tourists all year round. Located just 30 kilometres from Salzburg and 180 kilometres from Munich, Berchtesgaden is easily accessible. It is surrounded by Mount Watzmann, Germany's third highest mountain, the Kehlstein and nearby is the glacial lake of Königssee. There are a variety of sights and sports to be either watched or tried at all times of the year, whatever the weather. In summer the area is popular for walking and hiking and in winter you can try almost every winter sport imaginable including skiing, bobsleigh and snow shoe walking. The Berchtesgaden area is an ideal holiday destination, whether you are a couple looking for a peaceful, picturesque location or a family who wants to make the most of the sights and the sports that are on offer.

All the detailed information you need is here about restaurants, sports, sightseeing and the history of the area. This is a must have volume for anyone really wanting to make the most of their Alpine holiday.